SPLASH ZONE

Leader's Guidebook

KAZUKO SHIKUMA

Book Vine Press
2516 Highland Dr.
Palatine, IL 60067

CONTENTS

ACKNOWLEDGEMENTS

When I was pregnant with my daughter, I met Daphne Kirk, the founder of Generation2generation. Daphne Kirk taught about reconnecting the generations and equipping children "together." She introduced "intergenerational small groups," small groups built of families with children.

When my daughter was about a year old, my husband and I led our first "intergenerational small group." Since then we have had the privilege of leading multiple small groups with families with young children. My daughter grew up surrounded by people who love the LORD which help lay a firm foundation of faith within her. The tools you will see in this book work—they help us reconnect the generations.

I would like to thank all the families that were part of our "intergenerational small groups" in Pleasanton and families such as the Gonzales, Vierra, and Zirpolo families, who have graciously opened their homes to host the meetings week after week. *Splash Zone* would never have been born without their hospitality. Also I would like to express how grateful I am for Bridget and Amel, the Ngs and the Hermanns, who have joined us to raise our children *"together."* We will always cherish and remember the times we worked together to overcome the challenges that we faced that were unique to our endeavor. I am forever grateful for all of you who have been a part of God's plan to connect the generations. I will never forget the days we laughed, cried, and prayed with our children.

Special thanks to Elliot, Michelle, and Terry, who have given me feedback regarding the content; Larry and Lois Hino for their prayers; and all of my precious friends for their encouragement. I am grateful beyond words for Isabel, who offered the illustrations, and Axel, both of whom have spent many hours meeting with me to format *Splash Zone Leader's Guidebook* and *Splash Zone Children's Activity Book.*

I am grateful to my husband Ted, who has responded to God's calling to lead small groups with families with young children and has been supportive of this project. I would not have been able to write a single page without his loving support. I am also grateful to my daughter Naomi, who has spent six years of her life in small groups with children and is now growing in her teenage years with the fear of God in her heart. I also would like to give honor to my father, who always encouraged me to finish what I started, and my mother, who taught me what it means to serve others with love.

I dedicate *Splash Zone* to my loving Savior, who led me and guided me years before I came up with the idea of publishing this book. I acknowledge that without Him, *Splash Zone* would not have been published. Every time I doubted myself or thought of putting this project aside, He always encouraged me through people, visions, and in dreams to keep writing and not give up.

INTRODUCTION

God, by His infinite wisdom, invented the generations.

"Forever" is one of the phrases in the Bible at which we often glance. It is difficult for us to fathom "forever," a time with no end. Yet the Bible mentions a type of time that has no end, demonstrated on this earth.

"He remembers his covenant FOREVER." (Psalm 111:Sb)
"The LORD is faithful forever." (Psa lm 117 :2)
"His faithful love continues forever." (Psalm 136:1b)

How can God be praised forever, and how can His love be demonstrated on this earth forever?

One day I was at a grocery store, watching people go by with carts full of items and their children sitting in their carts. During this somewhat mundane moment, God showed me His heart for the generations. As I watched the children sitting in the carts and parents who were raising them pass by, I realized that I was seeing the generations pass by - one generation to the next generation. That moment God showed me that the generation was His invention - He created the generations.

I understood that only through the generations can we make evident the reality of God's infinity on earth. His name will be glorified, on this earth beyond our time, when we choose to share the love we have encountered within our lifetime with the next generation. God, by His grace, has given us a privilege to be a part of this ongoing legacy.

The privilege of passing the baton to the next generation is given not only to the ones who have children, but also to those who are single or who do not have children. In Luke 8, Jesus states that whoever longs to hear God's Word and puts it into practice is like His family. We understand from this statement that, whether we have children or not, we are part of the greater family- and families raise children together. When we choose to be a part of His family and to nurture our children, God will grow them.

Splash Zone has been born from God's heart for the generations - His love for those who have gone before us, for those who are to come, and for those of us who are living out their destiny right now. Splash Zone is a tool to connect the generations. It is also a resource for leaving a legacy that will last beyond the time we have on earth - from generation to generation.

CHILDREN AND SMALL GROUPS

When it comes to small group Bible studies, most of us dismiss children as members of the small group. Parents with young children give up attending small groups for a few years until their children are able to stay home by themselves. When children tag along, they end up sitting in front of a screen.

Deep inside, we all feel a little guilty for having our children go through this ritual week after week during Bible studies. Why? It is because we all know that children, as well as adults, need to be fed by the Word, and they can benefit from being a part of a community.

UNIQUE FEATURES OF *SPLASH ZONE*

Splash Zone is a curriculum that can be used by any adults in a Bible study group to lead the children in their small group settings. The guide book will help the adults in the small group to take turns leading the children nurture them by the Word of God. *Splash Zone* can also be used as a curriculum for Sunday Schools, Vacation Bible Schools, or Bible study guide for families.

Requires minimal preparation

With *Splash Zone*, any adult in the group can lead children in a small group without scrambling to find craft items. Suggested answers to every question asked and Scripture passages are there in this Guidebook.

Promotes interaction and builds relationships

Splash Zone has a one-of-a-kind approach that helps build relationships with children while introducing them to Biblical principles. The leader's guidebook is filled with thought-provoking questions and lessons designed to help you interact with children.

Encourages children to spend time in the Word of God

In *Splash Zone,* children will be splashed by the Word of God every week. The Word of God nourishes our spirits. Children need this food as much as we do. The Word of God – substance of their faith.

Brings life to the Word

Real-life testimonies give life and richness to the Word of God. In *Splash Zone,* you are encouraged to share your own testimonies with the children. In the "Listen and Ask" sections, for example, you will see two or three sentences for you to complete. The sentences are there to assist you in sharing your own stories with the children.

Suggests interactive games

One of the ways to build relationships with children is to play together. There are three non-active games and one indoor-friendly active game listed in each lesson. The supplies required for these games are minimal, often only sheets of paper, crayons, and pencils. Feel free to improvise and adapt the games to the needs of your group.

May God bless you richly as you lead the children in your small group and pass your baton to the next generation through *Splash Zone*.

PSALM 78

My people, listen to my teaching.
Pay attention to what I say
I will open my mouth and tell stories.
I w!II speak about things that were hidden.
They happened a long time ago.
We have heard about them and we know them
Our people who lived before us have told us about them.
We won't hide them from our children.
We will tell them about what the Lord has done that is worthy of praise.
We will talk about hispower and the wonderful things he has done.
He gave laws to the people of Jacob.
He gave Israel their law.
He commanded our people who lived before us to teach his laws to their children.
Then those born later would know hislaws.
Even their children yet to come would know them.
And theyin turn would tell their children. Then they would put their
trust in God They would not forget what he has done.
They would obeyhiscommands.
They would not be /Jke their people who lived before them.
Those people were stubborn. They refused to obey God
Their hearts were not true to him. Their spirits were not faithful to him.

RUNNING A SMALL GROUP WITH CHILDREN

Here is a simple structure that anyone (adults and children) can follow to move small groups with children along.

The Four Ws

The format consists of four Ws; Welcome, Worship, Word, and Witness. Follow the Four Ws. Take turns leading one of the Ws each month. Rotating responsibilities will give everyone in the group the opportunity to lead all of the four vt,s and be equipped to lead a new group when God calls them to. (note: The four Ws is a format introduced by Daphne Kirk in her book Heirs togetherp.39–p.43.)

Welcome (20min.): Demonstrate hospitality.
Visit before the meeting (10min.)

- As the families gather, greet each other and welcome new people.
- Encourage children to greet people and be hospitable.

Open the meeting (10min.)

- Acknowledge Jesus as the center of the meeting.
- Address children every week, reminding them that they are a significant part of the group.
- Remind the adults that God has entrusted them with the children in the group.
- Explain the four 1,1.,s.
- Ask icebreaker questions.

Worship (10min.): Adults and children worship together.

- Ask someone in the group to lead worship ahead of time.
- Have the children pick their favorite worship songs.

Word (50min.): Children will go to a separate room (to the "Splash Zone").

- *Splash Zone* can be led by any adult in the group at any time, but it is recommended that one person lead each unit (one month) to build relationships with the children.
- Children will use their *Splash Zone Chtldrens Activity Book*.
- Keep sheets of paper, crayons, and pencils at hand for activities and games.

Witness (10min.): Children will rejoin the adults.
Time of sharing (5min.)

- Children share what they have learned or show what they have completed in their activity books.
- If appropriate, adults share with the children what they have learned.

Prayer (5min.)

- Ask children and adults for prayer requests.
- Encourage children to lead in prayer as they feel comfortable.
- Pair children with adults other than their parents and pray for one another.

Close the meeting.

CURRICULUM OVERVIEW

Two books

- Guidebook for leaders. *(Splash Zone Leader's Guidebook)*
- Activity book for each child. *(Splash Zone Children's Activity Book)*

Ten units to cover ten months/year

- *Splash Zone* consists of ten units (one unit/month). This allows your small group to take two months off (one in summer and one in winter) each year.

Three lessons in each unit

- There are three lessons in each unit (three lessons/month).
- Have a fun night on the fourth week of the month (or twice in a month if there are five weeks that month)

Fun nights

- Fun night can be a game night, a movie night, a birthday party (any type of celebration), a talent show, a pool party, an outing or any activity a family would do for fun together!
- Share a meal - set up potluck on some of the fun nights.
- Fun nights help build relationships with people (adults and children) in the group.

Supplies needed for Splash Zone

- *Splash Zone Chtfdren 's Activity Book*
- sheets of paper
- crayons
- pencils
- masking tape (for some games)

WORKSHOP INFORMATION

- If you would like to host a workshop to make grater use of Splash Zone, please contact kakuma.art@gmail.com for more information

ADDITIONAL RESOUCRES

- *Reconnecting the Generations* by Daphne Kirk
- *Heirs Together establishing intergenerational Church* by Daphne Kirk
- *The Chtfd's Story Bible* by Catherine F. Vos

LESSON OVERVIEW

1. ATTENDANCE PAGE

- In the *Splash Zone Ch!ldren's Activity Book*, you will find the "Splash Zone Attendance" page.
- Children will each earn one sticker on a lily pad (or color one of the lily pads) when they attend Splash Zone.
- There are lily pads with "Get a Prize" for every five attendance.
- When a child reaches "Get a Prize," reward the child with a small toy (or any prize your group decides).
- Tip: Keeping prizes in a "special box" is always fun!

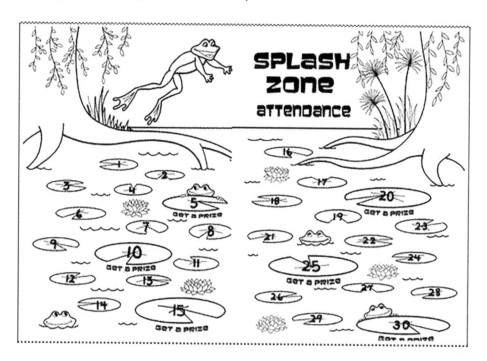

2. WELCOME

- In each lesson, you will find a few questions you can ask the children to help you build relationships with them.
- In this section you will also find an "Icebreaker Question" that is designed to help the children regroup for the lesson.
- In each lesson you are encouraged to share your own answers with the children.
- You can also encourage the children to be creative and come up with their own icebreaker questions.

3.   BOOKS OF THE WEEK

- This section is designed to help children familiarize themselves with the books of the Bible by reciting and memorizing them.

- Reward children by putting a sticker on their Children's Activity Book when they have tried their best to recite and memorize the books of the Bible.

- Suggested format for memorization.
  1.   **Introduce the books/Review the Books**
  2.   **Pick one memorization exercise**

- In each lesson you will find three types of repetition that help children memorize the names of the books.

a. Repeat in groups

Get in smaller groups and take turns saying the names of the books.

> Example: Group A: Genesis, Exodus
>
> Group B: Leviticus, Numbers

<u>Variations</u>

> Switch roles.
> Change the tempo: fast, slow, or extremely fast/slow.
> Change your voice: high pitch, low pitch, soft, loud.
> Change the size: from groups of five down to pairs

b. Say them like a _____.

Pick a character, an animal, occupation or a celebrity and say the names of the books in their voices.

c. Keep the beat

Have the children say the books of the week to a beat. (There are apps you can use to help you with the beat.)
<u>Variations</u>
> Change tempo: fast, slow, or extremely fast/slow.
> Change rhythm. Recite with eyes closed.

d. Skip repetition

One well-known game using this technique is "Head, shoulders, knees and toes." If you have ever played "Head, shoulders, knees, and toes," you would know exactly how this works.

Skip repetition is also called "inner-hearing." As you skip one word within a sequence of words, the skipped word gets amplified in the brain. When you skip the word, you are actually repeating the word in your mind, and the word gets reinforced in memory.

Example:
Leader: "Genesis, Exodus, Leviticus, Numbers."
Children: "Genesis, Exodus, Leviticus, Numbers."

Leader skips the first one: "(clap), Exodus, Leviticus, Numbers."
Children skip the first one: "(clap), Exodus, Leviticus, Numbers."

Leader skips the second one: "Genesis, (clap), Leviticus, Numbers."
Children skip the second one: "Genesis, (clap), Leviticus, Numbers."

c. Recording session
Record the recitation and listen to the recordings! Create a video clip!

4. WORD

- In this section, you will see series of questions that will help you share Biblical concepts with the children.

- Questions in "The Lesson" are designed to guide and encourage children to apply Biblical principles to their life.

- Your group will have children with different needs (ages will vary, for example). Feel free to improvise, skip, or even change the questions to accommodate the need of children in your group.

5. ACTIVITIES

- Activity pages that are in the children's workbook are the pages on which children draw or write about what they have learned.

- These pages reinforce what they have learned in "WORD."

- In each lesson there is an illustration related to the lesson.

- Have the children color in the pictures as you teach, during activities, or after the games.

6. SHARE WITH THE CHILDREN

- In this section you will find open-ended questions prompting you to share your own experience or testimony with the children with your own words.

- Bring life to the Word.

- Help children apply what they have learned to their own lives.

7. GAMES

- In this section you will find games to play with children.

Instructions for the Games

Card Games

You Will need a deck of cards.

- Card games are always fun and easy to play.
- Bring out a set of playing cards and share your favorite card games with the children!

Draw it! [Can be played in teams or individually.]

You will need paper and a pen or pencil

OBJECTIVE OF THE GAME to guess the word given to a person/team to draw.

- Pick one word from the list provided in the lesson.
- Pick one person to draw the word or a phrase chosen by the player or the leader.
- Have the other players or team members guess the word or phrase.

Add more fun!

Use a timer to limit the time of drawing.

Who am I? [Played individually.]

You Will need paper, pen or pencil, tape

OBJECTIVE OF THE GAME to guess who you are with the least number of questions.

- Have the children pick a name or an object from the theme listed in the lesson and write it down on a small piece of paper.
- Tape the name on the back of another person.
- Have each child go around the room and ask yes or no questions about the name on his or her back.
- The person who has guessed his or her name in the least number of questions wins.

Draw for the Master   [Can be played in teams or individually.]

You Will need   paper and a pen or pencil

OBJECTIVE OF THE GAME   to guess the word given to a person/team to draw.

- Choose one person to be the Master.
- Give one player or team a piece of paper and pencil.
- Assign a phrase from the list in each lesson to the player/team.
- Have the player/team draw the phrase and show it to the Master.
- Have the Master decode the picture.
- If the Master cannot figure out the phrase, another person/team will take up the mission of drawing the sentence.
- You can create sentences for children to draw.

Add more fun!

Have the children come up with phrases to draw for the Master.

The Guardian   [Can be played in teams

You Will need   a bowl/container, a chair, a set of keys, a paper sword (rolled newspaper)

OBJECTIVE OF THE GAME   to get the keys from the bowl under the Guardian and back to where he/she started without being hit.

- Arrange the children in a wide circle and set a chair in the center.
- Put a set of keys in a bowl, and place it under the chair.
- Pick one person to be the Guardian of the keys.
- Blindfold the Guardian.
- The Guardian will sit on the chair and have a paper sword (rolled newspaper).
- Players will try to get the keys from the bowl without being hit by the guardian.
- If a person is hit, he/she is out.
- A person who has accomplished the mission gets to be the next Guardian.

Add more fun!

Turn the light off and play in the dark.

I Found My Dentures!   [Played in one group.]

talk without showing teeth.

- Everyone sits in a circle.
- During this game, players must cover their teeth with their lips and not show their teeth.
- Pick a category such as animals, fruits, vegetables, fast-food restaurants or animation characters.
- Each player will choose a word within the category.
- The first player will say the word he or she has picked, still covering teeth with lips. Example: The first player says, "Carrot, carrot."
- The second player will say the word the first player has picked and the one he/she has picked. Example: The second player says, "carrot, carrot, broccoli, broccoli."
- The third player will say the word the second player has picked and the one he/she has picked. Example: The third player says, "Broccoli, broccoli, tomato, tomato."
- If you see someone's teeth, you alert the group by calling out "I found my dentures!"
- The person who showed teeth will be eliminated and game will continue going around the circle until one person remains.

Masking Tape Activities   [Can be played in teams or individually.]

   a roll of masking tape.

Standing long jump
- Place masking tape on floor to draw a line.
- Have a person stand on the line and jump as far as he or she can.
- Each child will take turns jumping as for as possible.

Ready, Aim, Roll
- Tape a bull's eye on the floor.
- Tape a straight line to mark where the ball will be rolled from.
- Have each child roll the ball from the line.
- Write the points on the masking tape and compete.

Masking Tape Hop-Scotch
- Tape a hop-scotch pattern on the floor and play.

Mission "Balance"   [Can be played in teams or individually.]

You Will need   three or four items that are safe to balance on head.

OBJECTIVE OF THE GAME   to walk a course without dropping an item balanced on the head.

- Pick a starting line and a finish line in the room.
- Have a player (or a person from a team) pick an item to balance on his or her head.
- Have the person walk from the starting line to the finish line without dropping the item.
- The next player (or a person from another team) will take up the challenge and do exactly the same as the first player.
- If the player walks the course without dropping the item, that person (or the team) wins and will pick the next item.

Add more fun!

Create a course around furniture.

Paper Planes   [Can be played in teams or individually.]

You Will need   sheets of paper

- Each person receives a sheet of paper.
- Have each person fold his or her paper to make an airplane.
- Fly the airplanes and have fun!

Add more fun!

Draw on the paper plane. Measure how far the plane flew.
Try to make the plane land close to a mark and measure how close the plane landed. Add the distance and compete between teams.

Paper Dash   [Can be played in teams or individually.]

You Will need   two sheets of paper

OBJECTIVE OF THE GAME   to get to the finish line only by stepping on the two pieces of paper. The player who finishes the course in the shortest time wins.

- Pick a starting line and a finish line in the room.
- Players are given two pieces of paper and line up at the start.
- Measure time taken to reach the goal.

Add more fun!

Create a course around furniture.

"Scene 1, Take 1"   [Can be played in teams or individually.]

OBJECTIVE OF THE GAME   to act out a word or a phrase and have others guess the word.

- Pick one word from the list provided in the lesson.
- Pick one person to act out the word or a phrase.
- Have the other players guess the word or phrase.
- You can form a group, or play individually.
- Use a timer to limit the time of miming.

The Secret Object   [Can be played in teams or individually.]

OBJECTIVE OF THE GAME   to guess the object within twenty questions.

- Pick one player to be the "Answerer."
- The "Answerer" chooses a secret object.
- The "Questioners" take turns asking "yes" or "no" questions of the "Answerer" to figure out what the secret object is.
- The Questioner who guesses the secret object becomes the "Answerer" for the next round.
- If the "Questioners" fails to guess the secret object within twenty questions, the "Answerer" gets to choose another secret object.

Super Toes   [Can be played in one group or teams.]

OBJECTIVE OF THE GAME   to pass a small object between people with toes.

- All players sit in a circle or a line.
- Pick a small object for the children to pass from one person to the next with their toes.
- Time how long it takes to pass the item around the circle.
- You can challenge the children to cut their time.
- You can also have two or more groups of children race.

Telephone   [Played in teams.]

OBJECTIVE OF THE GAME   to pass the message correctly.

- Have the children sit in one or two lines.
- The leader chooses a phrase listed in each lesson.
- The leader whispers the phrase to the first child in line.
- Have the first child whisper the phrase to the next child and so on.
- Have the last child say the phrase out loud.
- The team that has passed the message correctly wins.

Where is the delivery?   [Played in one group.]

OBJECTIVE OF THE GAME   to pass the object without being detected.

- Sit close together in a circle.
- Pick one person to sit in the middle to figure out where the delivery item is.
- Pick a small item to pass around behind the circle.
- Have the person in the middle find the item.

1.1 THE BIBLE
THE MOST AMAZING BOOK IN THE WORLD!

Welcome

5'

Find out about the children. Share your answers first.

- What was the best thing that happened this week?
- What was the best gift you had ever received?
- Find out about the gift-who did you receive it from and why you like that gift.

Icebreaker   Share your answers first.

- If you could give any gift to your parents, what would it be and why?

Books of the Week

Name The Books

5'

GENESIS
EXODUS
LEVITICUS
NUMBERS

Process

TEACHER	STUDENTS
1) Introduce the Books 2) Repeat in groups 3) Skip repetition 4) Keep the beat	Say the names of the books in the Bible by yourself and get a sticker!

STICKER PLEASE...

It is important for children not only to know what the Bible is, but also to hear how the Bible has influenced your life.

The Lesson

Today we are going to talk about the Bible.

o   Have each child hold the Bible.

Would you please share what you know about the Bible?

o   Have the children share what they know about the Bible.

In the Psalms, David wrote…

"The law of the LORD is perfect 11 (Psalm 19:7)

"The LORD's word doesn't have any flaws." (Psalm 18:30)

This means that God's Word in the Bible is perfect and that the promises that are written in the Bible are true. The Bible is a gift from God to his people.

God spoke to His people and told them to write down the words He has spoken to them. Paul said in 2Timothy 3:16 that

"God has breathed life into all of Scripture."

What do you think, "God has breathed life into all of Scripture" mean?

o   Have the children share their thoughts.

•   It means that it has been written by the Holy Spirit, the breath of God.

•   God Himself wrote them through people who love God.

The Bible is a library of many kinds of books. What kinds of books do you think are in this library?

o   Allow children to guess freely and let them have fun guessing.

•   There are books of history, laws, letters, songs, proverbs, and so on.

There are two major parts in the Bible. Can you guess what they are?

o   Allow children to guess freely and have fun guessing.

•   Two major parts of the Bible are the Old Testament and the New Testament.

Can you guess how many books are in the Old Testament?

- ○ Allow children to guess freely and have fun guessing.

- • There are thirty-nine books in the Old Testament.

- • The four books we recited today are the first four books of the Old Testament.

Can you guess how many books are in the New Testament?

- ○ Allow children to guess freely and have fun guessing.

- • There are twenty-seven books in the New Testament (sixty-six books in all).

What is so special about the sixty-six books in the Bible?

- ○ Have the children share their thoughts.

- • They were all inspired (encouraged to write) by the Spirit of God.

- • God is the ultimate author of all the books in this library.

- • God wrote it through His people.

- • The books are perfect truth, unlike any other writings.

- • "The word of God is alive and active." (Hebrews 4:12)

- • Bible is useful for everyone-past, present, and future.

Guess how many people wrote the Bible?

- ○ Allow children to guess freely and have fun guessing.

- • About forty people from different times and places.

- • This library of books is the world's all-time bestseller and the world's most translated book.

When Jesus was tempted by the devil, He answered and said,

"It is written, 'Man must not live only on bread He must also live on every word that comes from the mouth of God'"(Matthew 4:4-5).

What do you think this means?

- ○ Have the children share their thoughts.

- • Just as our body needs food to stay healthy and grow, our soul needs nourish ment as well.

- • Reading the Bible is absolutely necessary for the health of your souls.

The Bible is a book that you are going to read for the rest of your life. You will not get bored of it because you will find something new every time you read it. You are going to read the books in the Bible over and over.

- • The more you read it, the wiser you become.

- • The more you read it, the happier you will become.

- • The more you read it, the more you will be equipped to tackle things that you face in life.

5'

Draw a line to a number

3   66   4

How many Books are in the Old Testament?

39   How many Books are in the New Testament?

27   15

How many Books are in the Bible?   20

DRAW A PICTURE

Draw a picture of yourself reading a Bible.

Below are sentences for YOU to complete and share with the children. Pick one or two of them and share your own thoughts with the children. Ask the Holy Spirit and share appropriate examples or your testimonies.

- I read the Bible because…

- My favorite book in the Bible is _____ because… (explain why)

- My life would be different if I did not read the Bible.
  (Explain how your life would be different without reading the Bible by sharing an appropriate story.)

Fun Time

Games

10+

- **"Scene 1, Take 1"**

   an ant, someone praying, bees flying, someone playing a harp, The Bible, a bird, earrings, fire, wind, cloud, walk on the water, a person singing, a door, chains, a key, an apple

- **Draw for the Master**

   a corn on a chair, a bat flying over a road, a rabbit in a pocket, a sandwich under a tall ladder, a tiger crossing a bridge,
  a watermelon and carrots in a basket, a fox lying on a bed

- **The Secret Object**

- **Paper Dash**

Notes

1.2 THE BIBLE
THE OLD TESTAMENT

Welcome

Find out about the children. Share your answers first.

- Ask children what they did during the week.
- Find out what animals children like and why.
- Find out if the children have pets, and how they feel about them.

Icebreaker   Share your answers first.

- If you could be any animal, what would you like to be and why?

Name The Books

DEUTERONOMY

JOSHUA

JUDGES

RUTH

Process

TEACHER	STUDENTS
1) Introduce the Books 2) Say them like a _____ 3) Repeat in groups 4) Skip repetition	Say the names of the books in the Bible by yourself and get a sticker!

Word: Lesson Objectives

20'

It is essential for children to know how you value the Word of God. Share how the Old Testament has influenced *your* life.

The Lesson

Last week we talked about the Bible. How many books are in the Old Testament?

- There are thirty-nine books.

We recited eight of those books so far. Can you say them?

- Genesis, Exodus, Leviticus, Numbers, Deuteronomy, Joshua, Judges, Ruth

Can you guess who wrote the first five books?

- ○ Accept guesses from children.

- Moses wrote the first five books. "The first five books are called the Pentateuch.
- ○ Have the children say "Pentateuch." [pen-tuh-took]

What do you think the five books were written about?

- ○ Have the children share their thoughts.

- The first five books were the Law (Torah) given to us by God.

What do you think the laws were for?

- ○ Have the children share their thoughts.

- The laws were given by God so people who follow God will live as God wants them to live.

The next group of books is the "Prophets." What is a prophet?

- ○ Have the children share their thoughts.

- A prophet is one who speaks forth messages.

What do you think prophets in the Bible spoke?

- ○ Have the children share their thoughts.

- Bible prophets spoke forth what they heard from God the Creator.

Let's see how many prophets we can name together.

- ○ Have the children look at their Bible and share their thoughts.

- Hosea, Amos, Joel, Jonah, Isaiah, Jeremiah, Obadiah, Micah, Nahum, Habakkuk, Zephaniah, Ezekiel, Daniel, Haggai, Zechariah, and Malachi are the prophets.

The Lesson

In the Old Testament days, people who did not believe a prophet or disobeyed a prophet's words were counted as those who had disbelieved or disobeyed God.

Deuteronomy 18:19 says,

"The prophet wt!/ speak in my name. But someone might not listen to what I say through the prophet Then I will hold that person responsible for not listening."

The next books are called history books. History is a record of past events.
Can you guess which ones are the history books?
- o   Have the children open their Bibles.
- o   Allow children to guess freely and have fun guessing.
- •   Joshua, Judges, Ruth, 1 Samuel, 2 Samuel, 1 Kings, 2 Kings, 1 Chronicles, 2 Chronicles, Ezra, Nehemiah, and Esther are the history books.

The next books are poetry and wisdom books. Pick one book from the Bible that you think might be a poetry and wisdom book.
Can you guess which ones are poetry and wisdom books?
- o   Allow children to guess freely and have fun guessing.
- •   Job, Psalms, Proverbs, Ecclesiastes, and Song of Solomon are the poetry and wisdom books.

Let's play a game! Can you think of stories in the Old Testament?
- •   Play 'True or False."
- •   Example; "David and Goliath is written in the New Testament. True or False?"

Old Testament Stories	New Testament Stories
Noah and the Ark,	Feeding of the Five Thousand,
The Crossing of the Red Sea,	Jesus Walking on Water,
The Battle of Jericho,	Wind and Waves Obey Jesus,
David and Goliath,	John Baptizes Jesus,
The Fiery Furnace,	Parable of the Mustard Seed,
Daniel in the Lion's Den,	Resurrection of Lazarus,
Esther Made Queen	Saul Blinded for Three Days

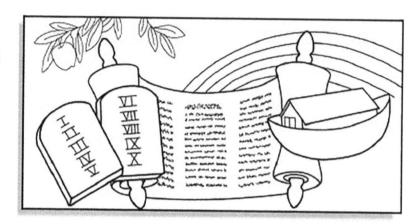

DRAW A PICTURE

Draw a picture of one of the stories in the Old Testament that you know.

Share With the Children

Below are sentences for YOU to complete and share with the children. Pick one or two of them and share your own thoughts with the children. Ask the Holy Spirit and share appropriate examples or your testimonies.

- My favorite story in the Old Testament is _____ because...
  (How did the story affect the way you think, or the way you live?)

- My favorite character in the Old Testament is _____ because...

- I like the book of _____ because...

Games

Fun Time

- **"Draw it"**

   feet, a baby, the Ark, a giant, thunder, a tree, a shepherd, an egg, a cup, a chair, a fire engine, an airplane, a window, a bird, an ice cream cone

- **Who/What am I?**

   Animals: a dog, a bat, a camel, a monkey, a crab, a donkey, an elephant, a frog, an owl, a shark, a turtle, a woodpecker, a snake, a rabbit

- **Card Games**

- **Where is the delivery?**

Notes

1.3 THE BIBLE
THE NEW TESTAMENT

Find out about the children. Share your answers first.

- Ask the children what they did during the week.
- Find out the children's favorite fruit and why.
- Find out if they have ever harvested any fruit. Ask if they liked it or not.

Icebreaker   Share your answers first.

- If you could be a fruit, what fruit would you like to be and why?

Books of the Week

Name The Books

5'

GENESIS, EXODUS, LEVITICUS, NUMBERS, DEUTERONOMY, JOSHUA, JUDGES, RUTH

Process

TEACHER

1) Review the Books
2) Ask for a volunteer to recite alone or with friends
3) Encourage & reward!

STUDENTS

Say the names of the books in the Bible by yourself and get a sticker!

STICKER PLEASE...

Word: Lesson Objectives

It is essential for children to know how *you* are captivated by the Word of God. Share how the New Testament influenced your life.

The Lesson

How many books are in the New Testament?
- ° Allow children to guess freely and have fun guessing.
- • There are twenty-seven books in the New Testament.

Where does the New Testament begin?
- ° Have the children open their Bibles and explore.

Can you guess what the first four books in the New Testament are called?
- ° Accept guesses from children.
- • They are called the four Gospels.

What are the names of the four Gospels?
- ° Have the children find out by looking at their Bibles.
- • Matthew, Mark, Luke, and John are the four Gospels.

Can you guess what the four Gospels are about?
- ° Allow children to guess freely and have fun guessing.
- • They are biographies (life stories) of Jesus.
- • They tell about the birth, life, death, and resurrection of Jesus.

Where is the book of Acts?
- ° Have the children find the book of Acts and open to Acts.
- ° Read Acts 1 :1-2a:
  "Theoph!lus, I wrote about Jesus in my earlier book I wrote about all he did and taught untll the day he was taken up to heaven."

Can you guess who wrote this book? Luke or Paul?
- ° Accept guesses from children.
- • Luke wrote to Theophilus.
- • "Theophilus" means lover of God.

What did Paul say he wrote about in the book of Acts?
- ° Have the children listen to the verse again and answer.
- • Paul said he wrote about all Jesus did and taught.

The Lesson

What do you think the book of Acts is about?
- ○ Have the children share their thoughts.
- • Acts is a book about people who changed the world by the power of the Holy Spirit.
- • Luke went on a voyage with Paul and wrote this book.
- • The book of Acts is a record of adventures Luke and Paul had while following the Holy Spirit.

Did you know that the book of Acts has not ended?
- • You and I are a part of this history book too, because God's Spirit is still working through us!

Can you guess which books are the letters Paul wrote to the churches?
- ○ Allow children to guess freely and have fun guessing.
- • Roman, 1 and 2 Corinthians, Galatians, Ephesians, Philippians, Colossians, 1 and 2 Thessalonians are the letters Paul wrote to the churches.

Why do you think Paul wrote these letters to the churches or his friends?
- ○ Have the children share their thoughts.
- ○ Share your thoughts with the children.

What is the last book of the Bible called?
- ○ Have the children find out by looking at the Bible.
- • The book of Revelation is the last book of the Bible.

What does "Revelation" mean?
- ○ Have the children share their thoughts.
- • "Revelation" means to expose, uncover, show, or display.

What do you think Revelation reveals (show us)?
- ○ Have the children share their thoughts.
- • There are two main things that are revealed. One is revelation given from Jesus and the other is revelation of Jesus.

Revelation says people who read or listen to this book are blessed (fortunate, lucky, happy).
- • It is a story of good King Jesus coming to rule the earth.
- • It is a book written to prepare the church for Jesus's return.
- • It is one of the most exciting books in the Bible.

DRAW A PICTURE

Draw a picture of one of the stories in the New Testament that you know about.

Share With the Children

5'

Below are sentences for YOU to complete and share with the children. Pick one or two of them and share your own thoughts with the children. Ask the Holy Spirit and share appropriate examples or your testimonies.

- My favorite story in the New Testament is _____ because...
  (How did the story affect the way you think, or the way you live?)

- My favorite character (besides Jesus) in the New Testament is _____ because...

- I like the book _____ because...

Fun Time

Games

10+

- **Telephone**

  - Every word of God is perfect.
  - At that time God's word came to John, son of Zechariah.
  - If you want something done right, you have to do it yourself.
  - Don't count your chickens before they are hatched.
  - You can lead a horse to water, but you can't make him drink.

- **Paper Planes**

- **I Found My Dentures!**

- **The Guardian**

Notes

2.1 GOD THE FATHER IS...
"OMNIPOTENT"—ALL POWERFUL

Welcome

Find out about the children. Share your answers first.

- Ask children what they did during the week.
- Find out children's favorite vehicles.
- Find out if they have ever been on it, and how it made them feel.

Icebreaker Share your answers first.

- If you could create a new vehicle, what would it be like?

Books of the Week

Name The Books

1ST & 2ND SAMUEL
1ST & 2ND KINGS
1ST & 2ND CHRONICLES

Process

TEACHER	STUDENTS
1) Review the Books 2) Repeat in groups 3) Skip repetition 4) Keep the beat	Say the names of the books in the Bible by yourself and get a sticker!

STICKER PLEASE...

Children think adults are powerful. It is important for children to know *you* (an adult) depend on God who is much more powerful than yourself.

The Lesson

<u>Today we are going to think about God's greatness.</u>

- The word people use to describe God's greatness is "omnipotent."
- ○ Have the children say "omnipotent." [om-nip-uh-tuh-nt]

Can you guess how it is spelled?

- ○ Have fun guessing how the word "omnipotent" is spelled.

Omnipotent means "all-powerful."

The prophet Jeremiah says to God,

"LORD and King, you have reached out your great and powerful arm. You have made the heavens and the earth. Nothing is too hard for you"(Jeremiah 32:17).

The angel Gabriel says to Mary,

"For with God nothing will be impossible." (Luke 1:37 NKJV).

Jesus says,

With God all things are possible"(Matthew 19:26).

Psalm 24:8 says:

"the LORD, who is strong and mighty. The LORD, who is mighty in battle."

Close your eyes as I read Psalm 24:8 one more time.

- ○ Read Psalm24:8 again.

How did you feel?

- ○ Have the children share how they felt.

Did you see anything?

- ○ Have the children share what they saw.

- God owns everything, and God is unbeatable.

Genesis 1:3 says:

"God said, 'Let there be light,' and there was light"

Is there anything in this world that has not been created by God?

- ○ Have the children share their thoughts.

- • There is nothing in this world that has not been created by God.

What did God create, and what did He use to create it?

- ○ Have the children share their thoughts.

- • God created everything from nothing.

Can we together list twenty things that God made?

- ○ Allow children to answer freely and have fun.

Psalm 24:1-2 says:

The earth belongs to the Lord And so does everything in it.
The world belongs to him. And so do all those who live in it.
He set it firmly on the oceans.
He made it secure on the waters.

Did God create the seas?

- • Yes, He did.

Who pushes back the oceans so that we are not flooded all the time?

- • God does.

Psalm 50:10-12 says:

Every animal in the forest already belongs to me.
And so do the cattle on a thousand hills.
I own every bird in the mountains.
The insects in the fields belong to me.
If I were hungry, I wouldn't tell you.
The world belongs to me. And so does everything in it.

Who does every animal in the world belong to?

- • Every animal belongs to God.

Why do they belong to God?

- ○ Have the children share their thoughts.

- • God owns everything because He created them first!

When someone makes or invents something for the first time, that person gets the credit and the idea will belong to that person.

What was the word that we use to say that God is all-powerful?

• Omnipotent.

God is powerful so He can do whatever He wills to do. Everything He does is out of Love. When we say God is omnipotent, we mean that God is able to do anything that aligns with His holy character.

Jesus said,

> *"No one is good but except God" (Mark 10:18)*

Numbers 23:19 says:

> *God isn't a mere human. He can't lie.*
> *He isn't a human being. He doesn't change his mind.*
> *He speaks, and then he acts.*
> *He makes a promise, and then he keeps it.*

Will God tell a lie or break His promises?

• No, He does not lie not break His promises.

Will God do anything sinful?

• No, He does not do anything sinful. He is powerful and always good.

How does "God being all-powerful" make you feel?

o Have the children share how they feel.
o Share how God's omnipotence make you feel.

Color the Picture

Activities

DRAW A PICTURE

Draw a picture of what God can do,

Below are sentences for YOU to complete and share with the children. Pick one or two of them and share your own thoughts with the children. Ask the Holy Spirit and share appropriate examples or your testimonies.

- Understanding the omnipotence of God helps me because...
- One time when I experienced God's omnipotence was...
- I think of God's omnipotence when...

Fun Time

Games

10+

- **"Scene 1. Take 1"**

 a sling shot, baking bread, a sheep drinking water, a fisherman, a carpenter, someone dreaming, someone standing on a rock.

- **Draw for the Master**

 lion delivering a dozen roses, someone running to deliver pizza, an eagle flying over a great waterfall, a person eating grapes at the beach

- **The Secret Object**

- **Masking Tape Activities**

2.2 GOD THE FATHER IS...
"OMNISCIENT"—ALL KNOWING

Welcome

5'

Find out about the children. Share your answers first.

- Ask children what they did during the week.
- Find out what each child's favorite cartoon character is and why.
- Find out how much time each child spend their time watching that cartoon.

Icebreaker   Share your answers first.

- If your favorite cartoon character came alive, what would you like to do with him or her?

Name The Books

5'

EZRA

NEHEMIAH

ESTHER

JOB

Process

TEACHER

1) Introduce the Books
2) Say them like a _____
3) Repeat in groups
4) Skip repetition

STUDENTS

Say the names of the books in the Bible by yourself and get a sticker!

Children think adults are powerful. It is important for children to know *you* (an adult) depend on God who is much more powerful than yourself.

The Lesson

Today we are going to think about how knowledgeable God is.

- The word people use to describe how God knows everything is "omniscient."
o Have the children say "omniscient." [om-nish-uh-nt]

Can you guess how it is spelled?

o Have fun guessing how the word "omnipotent" is spelled.

"Omniscient" means "knowing everything." Psalm 139:1 says:

you have seen what is in my heart Vou know all about me.

Does God know you?

- Yes

How much does He know about you?

o Have the children share their thoughts.

- God knows everything about us.

- He knows what I am thinking and feeling.

The next verse says,

You know when I sit down and when I get up.

Stand up. Does God know that you have just stood up?

- Yes.

Sit down. Does God know that you have just sat?

- Yes.

Does He know when you go to bed and when you wake up?

- Yes.

The verse continues,

> *You know what I am thinking even though you are far away*

Do you think a person can know what the other person is thinking?

- ○ Have the children share their thoughts.

- • A person may know what you are thinking sometimes, but not all the time. We can only guess.

Does God always know what a person is thinking?

- • Yes.

Psalm 139:3 says:

> *You know when I go out to work and when I come back home.*

Do you know what time I left my house this morning?

- ○ Allow children to guess freely and have fun guessing.

- • No. You might be able to guess, but you do not know for sure.

Does God know what time I left the house this morning?

- ○ Allow children to guess freely and have fun guessing.

- • Yes, and He knows it to the second.

Does he know what you were thinking when you went to bed last night?

- • Yes.

The verse continues, "You know exactly how I live."

What could this mean?

- ○ Have the children share their thoughts.

- • David says that God is familiar with everything you do.

- • God knows how you brush your teeth.

- • God also knows what is in your heart.

- • He knows when you are kind, polite, or respectful.

The Lesson

Psalm 139:4 says:

Lord, even before I speak a word, you know all about it

When someone is about to say something, would you know exactly what the person is going to say?

- ° Have the children share their thoughts.

- • We might be able to guess, but we do not know exactly what the person is going to say.

- • David says before we say anything, God knows what we are going to say.

Does God know what happened in the past?

- • Yes, He does.

Does he know what is going to happen in the future?

- • Yes, He does.

How does God knowing everything about you make you feel?

- ° o Have the children share how it makes them feel.
- ° o Share with children how the omniscience of God make you feel.

Jesus also knows about you because He is one with Father God. Matthew 9:4 says:

Jesus knew what they were thinking. So he said, "Why do you have evil thoughts in your hearts?"

There was also a time when Jesus knew exactly what people were talking about. Matthew 16:5-9 says:

The disciples crossed over to the other side of the lake. They had fo gotten to take bread 'Be careful," Jesus said to them. "Watch out for the yeast of the Pharisees and Sadducees." The disciples talked about this among themselves. They said, "He must be saying this because we didn't bring any bread" Jesus knew what they were saying. So he said, "Your faith is so small! Why are you talking to each other about having no bread?

Color the Picture

Activities

DRAW A PICTURE

Draw a picture or write how you feel about God knowing all about you.

Share With the Children

5'

Below are sentences for YOU to complete and share with the children. Pick one or two of them and share your own thoughts with the children. Ask the Holy Spirit and share appropriate examples or your testimonies.

- Understanding the omniscience of God helps me because _____.
- One time when I experienced God's omniscience, was…
- I think of God's omniscience when…

Fun Time

Games

10+

- **"Draw it"**

 meat, clouds, gold, rain, eagle, ladder, owl, leaf, fly, arrow, deer, Jonah, light, raisin, snow, beard, wash, pond, soap, car, sun, airplane

- **Draw for the Master**

 Fruit or vegetable: grapes, grapefruit, blueberry, broccoli, carrot, celery, onion, corn, cucumber, eggplant, cabbage, pear, pineapple, artichoke, strawberry, tomato, watermelon, pumpkin, peach, mushroom

- **Card Games**

- **Super Toes**

2.3 GOD THE FATHER IS...
"OMNIPRESENT"—EVERYWHERE

Welcome

Find out about the children. Share your answers first.

- Ask children what they did during the week.
- Find out when children's birthdays are.
- Find out what kind of cake each child had or what kind of cake each one likes.

Icebreaker Share your answers first.

- If you could throw a birthday party for someone, who would it be?
- What would the party look like?

Name The Books

Books of the Week

ESIS, EXODUS, LEVITICUS,
NUMBERS, DEUTERONOMY, JOSHUA,
JUDGES, RUTH, 1ST & 2ND SAMUEL,
1ST & 2ND KINGS, 1ST & 2ND CHRONICLES
EZRA, NEHEMIAH, ESTHER, JOB

Process

TEACHER

1) Review the Books
2) Ask for a volunteer to recite alone or with friends.
3) Encourage & reward!

STUDENTS

Say the names of the books in the Bible by yourself and get a sticker!

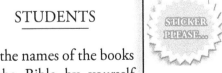

STICKER PLEASE...

Word: Lesson Objectives

Children need to know God is everywhere at all times. The assurance of this truth will help them stand on faith in God and stay strong.

Today we are going to talk about God's omnipresence.

- The word people use to describe how God is everywhere is "omnipresent."
- Have the children say "omnipresent." [om-nuh-prez-uh-nt]

Can you guess how it is spelled?

- Have fun guessing how the word "omnipresent" is spelled.

Have you ever traveled? How did you get there?

- Have the children share their traveling experiences.

Were you at home when you were there? Can we be in two places at the same time?

- No. We cannot be in two places at the same time.

Where is God?

- Have the children share their thoughts.

- Possible answers include the following: everywhere, in my heart, etc.

Does God know where we are?

- Yes. He is right with us even when we think we are hiding from Him.

Let's do an experiment.

- Have one child sit behind something so that other children cannot see him or her.

"We are not with [child's name] and we cannot see [child's name]."

Is God still with [child's name]? Can God see [child's name]?

- Yes. God can see [child's name] even when we cannot see [child's name]. We cannot be in two places at the same time.

Can God be in multiple places at the same time?

- Have the children share their thoughts.

- Yes, God can be in multiple places at the same time.

The Lesson

In Psalm 139 David wrote:

> *"You are all around me, behind me and in front of me"(v.5) "How can I get away from your Spirit? Where can I go to escape from you?" (v.7)*

David asked God many other questions like these.

How can a person get away from the Spirit of God?

○ Have the children answer David's question.

Where can a person go to hide from God?

○ Have the children answer David's question.

Can we go to a place where God cannot be?

• No, God can be in any place we choose to be.

Does God see us wherever we are?

○ Have the children share their thoughts.

• Yes, He sees us wherever we are.

• We cannot hide from God.

Why can't we hide from God?

○ Have the children share their thoughts.

• We cannot hide from God, because God is omnipresent (everywhere).

If we fly in airplanes or a space shuttle, can God be there?

○ Have the children share their thoughts.

• Yes, He can and will be there.

What if you lived underground? Would He find you there?

○ Have the children share their thoughts.

• Yes, He would find us.

• God is everywhere, and He is there and here right now.

Jesus said in Matthew 28:20,

> *"And you can be sure that I am always with you, to the very end"*

How does God being everywhere and right there with you make you feel?

○ Have the children share how God's omnipresence makes them feel.
○ Share with children how it makes you feel.

Proverbs 18:10 says:

> *"The name of the LORD is like a strong tower. Godly people run to it and are safe."*

When we run to God, who is powerful (omnipotent), knows everything (omniscient), and present everywhere (omnipresent), we are safe. We can run to Him because He knows everything about us and He is everywhere.

- ○ Note: Adam and Eve did the opposite. They hid from God.

We learned that God is everywhere, but there is one thing that can separate us from God.

What do you think that could be?

- ○ Have the children share their thoughts.

Hebrews 3:12 says:

> *"Brothers and sisters, make sure that none of you has a sinful heart Do not let an unbelieving heart turn you away from the living God 11*

According to this verse, what turns us away from God?

- ○ Have the children share their thoughts.

- • An unbelieving heart turns us away from God.

What is an unbelieving heart?

- ○ Have the children share their thoughts.

- • An unbelieving heart is a heart that is hard toward God.

An unbelieving heart can separate us from God. It is a heart that refuses to believe in the God who is omnipotent, omniscient, and omnipresent.

Color the Picture

Activities

DRAW A PICTURE

Draw a picture of Gof going everywhere with you. (school, home, shopping, underwater, mopuntains.)

Below are sentences for YOU to complete and share with the children. Pick one or two of them and share your own thoughts with the children. Ask the Holy Spirit and share appropriate examples or your testimonies.

- Understanding the omnipresence of God helps me because…

- One time when I experienced God's omnipresence, was…

- I think of God's omnipresence when…

Games

10+

- **"Telephone"**

  - Eating a good breakfast will help you wake up.
  - Fresh fruit is great for breakfast because it gives you vitamins you need from the beginning.
  - Jesus cooked the fish the disciples caught and said, "Come and have breakfast."
  - In everything, do to others what you would want them to do to you.

- **Paper Planes**

- **I Found My Dentures!**

- **Mission Balance**

3.1 MY FRIEND JESUS
HIS LIFE

Welcome 5'

Find out about the children. Share your answers first.

- Ask children what they did during the week.
- Find out what the children like to do other than watch TV or play games and why.
- Find out what their favorite things to do with their family or friends and why.

Icebreaker Share your answers first.

- Name one thing you would like to try if you had a chance and explain why you would like to try that.

Books of the Week

Name The Books 5'

PSALMS,
PROVERBS
ECCLESIASTES
SONG OF SOLOMON
ISAIAH

Process

TEACHER	STUDENTS
1) Introduce the Books 2) Repeat in groups 3) Skip repetition 4) Keep the beat	Say the names of the books in the Bible by yourself and get a sticker!

STICKER PLEASE...

Introduce Jesus and share how important He is to you.

The Lesson

<u>Today, we are going to talk about Jesus. What do you know about Jesus?</u>
- ○   Have the children share what they know.

Jesus was born in the town of Bethlehem.

Quiz time! What do you think Bethlehem means?
1. Does "Beth" mean lake, house, or dove?

   •   It means house.
2. Does "Le'chem" mean bread, fish, or water?

   •   It means bread.

   •   Bethlehem means "house of bread."

   When Jesus was little (about two years old), an angel warned his father, Joseph, to take him to Egypt, because King Herod was going to kill him. Joseph obeyed and went to Egypt.

How do you think they traveled to Egypt?
- ○   Have the children share their thoughts.

- •   They traveled on a donkey or walked.

How far do you think it is from Bethlehem to Egypt?
- ○   Allow children to guess freely and have fun guessing.

- •   It is about 350 miles.

How long do you think it might have taken for them to walk there?
- ○   Allow children to guess freely and have fun guessing.

- •   It takes about eighty-three hours to walk from Bethlehem to Egypt.

- •   If you start walking at eight o'clock in the morning and walk until three o'clock in the afternoon. It will take ten days to get there.

After some time, another angel appeared to Joseph and told him that they could go back to Nazareth. Jesus walked four hundred miles from Egypt to Nazareth when he was four or five years old!

What did Jesus's father, Joseph, do for a living?
- ○ Have the children share what they know.

- • He was a carpenter.

What do carpenters do?
- ○ Have the children share what they know.

- • Carpenters are people who are skilled in building ships or furniture out of wood.

Jesus grew up in Nazareth and learned his father's trade as a carpenter. What could he have built?
- ○ Have the children share their guesses.

What were the books in the Bible that are biographies of (books written about) Jesus?
- ○ Have the children share their guesses.

- • Matthew, Mark, Luke, and John.

When Jesus was thirty years old, he got baptized by his cousin.

Do you know the name of the person who baptized Jesus?
- ○ Have the children share their guesses.

- • John the Baptist baptized Jesus.

After he got baptized, Jesus selected his disciples.

How many of them do you think he picked?
- ○ Allow children to guess freely and have fun guessing.

- • Jesus picked twelve disciples.

- • He made road trips with his disciples and taught them many things.

What do you think he taught his disciples?
- ○ Have the children share their thoughts.

- • He taught them how to pray for the sick and taught them who God is.

- • He may have taught them fun games to play or taught them how to read, sing, cook, or even fish.

- • Jesus traveled with His disciples for three years.

At the last meal He had with the disciples, Jesus told them to share bread and wine to remember Him. This meal, which was a Passover dinner, is called the "Last Supper." He told his disciples to do the same even when He was gone to remember Him. That is what followers of Jesus do even today. Right after the Last Supper, Jesus was betrayed, then arrested, jailed, put on trial, falsely accused, convicted, beaten, humiliated, crucified, and buried after He died on the cross.

What happened after Jesus died?
o   Have the children share what they know.

•   Jesus was resurrected.

What does that mean?
o   Have the children share what they think it means.

•   It means that Jesus came back to life and that He is still alive.

When Jesus was resurrected, He showed Himself to more than five hundred people in forty days!

Where did Jesus go when forty days were over?
o   Have the children share their thoughts.

•   In Acts 1:9 it says,
"After Jesus said this, he was taken up to heaven. The apostles watched until a cloud hid him from their sight"

•   He ascended to heaven right in front of the disciples' eyes!

Where is He now?
o   Have the children share their thoughts.

•   In Mark 16:19 it says,
"When the Lord Jesus finished speaking to them, he was taken up into heaven. He sat down at the right hand of God"

•   He is in heaven, sitting at the right hand of the Father.

What is He doing there?
- ○ Have the children share their thoughts.

- • In Mark 8:34 it says,
  Christ Jesus is at the right hand of God and is also praying for us.

- • He is praying for us.

Who did Jesus send to be with us?
- ○ Have the children share their thoughts.

- • He sent the Holy Spirit to be with us.

Jesus said He was going to send the Holy Spirit, who would help us become more like Jesus.

What is going to happen next?
- ○ Have the children share their thoughts.

- • In Romans 5:17 it says,
  Those who receive the rich supply of God's grace w!l/ rule with Christ. The will rule in his kingdom.

  Jesus is going to come back on the clouds, He is going to rule the earth, and we are all going to work together with Him on this earth.

DRAW A PICTURE

Draw a picture of one of therese.

- Jesus making a table with his father.
- Jesus travelling with his disciples.
- Jesus on the cross.
- Jesus raised from the dead.
- Jesus taken up to heaven.
- Jesus coming back to earth to be with us.

Share With the Children

Below are sentences for YOU to complete and share with the children. Pick one or two of them and share your own thoughts with the children. Ask the Holy Spirit and share appropriate examples or your testimonies.

- I decided to follow Jesus because...
  (Share an appropriate occasion of how you decided to give your life to Jesus.)

- I know Jesus helps me because...

- The part in Jesus's life that encourages me the most is...

Games

10+

- **"Scene 1. Take 1"**

   a rooster on a table, cooking eggs, taking your shoes off, shopping at a grocery store, eating ice, drawing on paper, a bird eating a worm, walking in the rain

- **Draw fot the Master**

   someone eating spaghetti on a ship, salt and pepper on a picnic table, a person using a laptop in a park, chocolate covered marshmallows, doughnut on a flower plate

- **The Secret Object**

- **Paper Dash**

Notes

3.2 MY FRIEND JESUS
HE SAID, "BE BAPTIZED."

Welcome
5'

Find out about the children. Share your answers first.

- Ask children what they did during the week.
- Find out about children's family.
- Find out who they live with and where their extended families are.

Icebreaker   Share your answers first.

- If you could be any age, how old would you like to be and why?

Books of the Week

Name The Books
5'

JERENIAH
LAMENTATIONS
EZEKIEL

Process

TEACHER	STUDENTS
1) Review the Books 2) Ask for a volunteer to recite alone or with friends. 3) Encourage & reward!	Say the names of the books in the Bible by yourself and get a sticker!

STICKER PLEASE...

Word: Lesson Objectives

Introduce children to baptism.

The Lesson

Today we are going to talk about baptism. What do you know about baptism?
○   Have the children share what they know about baptism.

•   Baptism is when someone who is following Jesus goes into the water and then comes up again.

Listen to the story in Mark 1:9-11 and let's find out more about baptism.
○   Have the children listen to the story carefully.

> *At that time Jesus came from Nazareth in Galilee. John baptized Jesus in the Jordan River. Jesus was corning up out of the water. Just then he saw heaven being torn open. Jesus saw the Holy Spirit corning down on him like a dove. A voice spoke to him from heaven. It said, "You are my Son, and Ilove you. Iam very pleased with you'*

What did John do for Jesus?
○   Have the children share their thoughts.

•   He baptized Jesus.

•   Jesus was fully man and was obedient to receive baptism.

•   Baptism was a cleansing act, and Jews were following it for a long time.

What happened when Jesus came up out of the water?
○   Have the children share their thoughts.

•   The heavens opened, and the Holy Spirit came upon Him.

People who follow Jesus choose to be baptized because the Bible says it is Some thing Jesus did and He told us to do.

In Matthew 28:19-20, it is written that Jesus said:

> *So you must go and make disciples of allnations. Baptize them in the name of the Father and of the Son and of the Holy Spirit Teach them to obey everything Ihave commanded you. And you can be sure that Iamalways with you, to the very end.*

The Lesson

In Acts 2:38, it is written that Peter said:

> *All of you must turn away from your sins and be baptized in the name of Jesus Christ Then your sins wlfl be forgiven. You wlfl receive the gift of the Holy Spirit.*

What do we need to do before we are baptized?

- ○ Have the children share their thoughts.

- • We must turn away from our sins.

How did Jesus die?

- • He died on the cross.

- • Jesus died on the cross so that our sinful selves would have no power over us.

After He had died, His body was put into the tomb. Then what happened?

- ○ He came back to life.

Baptism shows that our old self died on the cross when Jesus died, that our old self has been buried, and that we have a new life just like Jesus was given a new life. We get baptized because it shows that the past is buried and that the new life has begun.

What part of baptism shows that a person has died with Jesus and has been buried?

- ○ Have the children share their thoughts.

- • When a person goes under the water in baptism, that indicates that the person has died and been buried.

What part of baptism shows that a person has a new life with God just like Jesus did?

- ○ Have the children share their thoughts.

- • When a person comes out of the water, it indicates that the person has new life.

Baptism is something you do when you truly believe in Jesus.

- • Baptism is saying publicly that you have made a decision to follow Jesus and will follow His ways for the rest of your life.

- • God will put the desire in your heart to be baptized one day.

- • When God puts a desire in your heart to be baptized, you should tell your parents, and they will help you out.

DRAW A PICTURE

Draw a picture of Jesus dying on the cross, buried, and coming back to life.

Draw a picture of someone being baptized.

Below are sentences for YOU to complete and share with the children. Pick one or two of them and share your own thoughts with the children. Ask the Holy Spirit and share appropriate examples or your testimonies.

- I was baptized (when, where and by whom.)
- I wanted to be baptized because…
- After being baptized, I felt…

Games

Fun Time

- **"Draw it"**

an apple, a wolf, wings, the Red Sea, a bird, a letter, bells, eating, tower of Babel, teeth, a wet towel, a baby in a basket, a torch, a shower, a dog

- **Who/What am I?**

Sweets: chocolate, caramel, cookies, chocolate chip, gummy bears, cupcakes, Ice cream, candy canes, gummy worms, bubble gums, jelly beans, brownies

- **Card Games**

- **Where is the delivery?**

Notes

3.3 MY FRIEND JESUS
HE SAID, "DO THIS." (COMMUNION)

Welcome

5'

Find out about the children. Share your answers first.

- Ask children what they did during the week.
- Find out about children's favorite bed time stories are and why.
- Find out children's favorite books.

Icebreaker Share your answers first.

- What character in your favorite story would you like to meet, and what do you think would be the first thing you would do or say when you meet the character?

Books of the Week

Name The Books

5'

, EXODUS, LEVITICUS NUMBERS,
DEUTERONOMY, JOSHUA, JUDGES, RUTH,
1ST & 2ND SAMUEL, 1ST & 2ND KINGS,
1ST & 2ND CHRONICLES, EZRA, NEHEMIAH, ESTHER, JOB,
PSALMS, PROVERBS, ECCLESIASTES, SONG OF SOLOMON,
ISAIAH, JEREMIAH, LAMENTATIONS, EZEKIEL

Process

TEACHER	STUDENTS
1) Introduce the Books 2) Say them like a _____ 3) Repeat in groups 4) Skip repetition	Say the names of the books in the Bible by yourself and get a sticker!

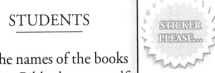

STICKER PLEASE...

Children are curious about Communion. It is important to share what it means to you so that they learn have reverence toward Communion.

The Lesson

Today we are going to learn about communion.
What is the most memorable meal you have had in your life? What made the meal so special?
- º   Share your answer first.
- º   Have the children share their answers.

Have you ever seen people take Communion?
- º   Have the children share their experiences.

- •   Communion is also called the Lord's Supper.

The Lord's Supper is a special meal Jesus had with His disciples before He died.

> When the Jewish people were slaves in Egypt, God's people cried out to God and asked Him to help them. God said He was going to send a judgment of death over Egypt. He told theIsraelites to slay an animal for their sins so that they would be protected from the judgment of their sins. They obeyed God and were protected.

> The meal the disciples had with Jesus was special to the Jewish people because it was a Passover meal where they remembered the Lamb slain for the sin of Israel.

What animal did God tell the Israelites to slay for their sins?
- º   Have the children share their thoughts.

- •   God told the Israelites to slay a lamb. The blood of this lamb was placed on their doorposts and death "passed over" them.

In Matthew 26:26-29 it says:

> Wh!le they were eating, Jesus took bread He gave thanks and broke it He handed it to his disciples and said, "Take this and eat it. This is my body." Then he took the cup. He gave thanks and handed it to them. He said, "All of you drink from it This is my blood of the covenant It is poured out to forgive the sins of many. Here is what I tell you. From now on, I won't drink wine with you again unt!l the day I drink it with you in my Father's kingdom."

Jesus took some bread and after blessing it He broke it.

What do you think the bread represents?
- ○ Have the children share their thoughts.

- • Breaking the bread represents the breaking of Jesus's (the Lamb's) body for our sins.

> After Jesus gave the bread for the disciples to eat, He took a cup with win and said, "This is my blood of the covenant. It is poured out to forgive the sins of many "(v27-28)

What do you think the wine represents?
- ○ Have the children share their thoughts.

- • It represents the pouring out of Jesus's blood for us.

Why do you think Jesus told us to take Communion?
- ○ Have the children share their thoughts.

- • He told us to take Communion so…
  We would remember that Jesus died for us.
  We would receive spiritual nourishment.
  We would know that we were a part of God's family.

Who should participate in the Lord's Supper?

º   Have the children share their thoughts.

1. Only those who believe in Christ should participate.

• Paul warns that those who eat and drink unworthily face serious consequences.

• 1 Corinthians 11:29–30 says:

Whoever eats and drinks must recognize the body of Christ If they don't, judgment w!II come upon them. That is why many of you are weak and sick. That is why a number of you have died

2. Only those who have examined themselves should participate.

• 1 Corinthians 11:27-28 says:

Eat the bread or drink the cup of the Lord in the right way Don't do it in a way that isn't worthy of him. If you do, you will be gUtlty. You'll be gUtlty of sinning against the body and blood of the Lord Everyone should take a careful look at themselves before they eat the bread and drink from the cup.

If you would like to take Communion, what should you do?

º   Have the children share their thoughts.

1. Ask your parents if you can take Communion.

2. Take it only when you understand why you are taking it.

3. Communion is not a snack time.

Color the Picture

Activities

DRAW A PICTURE

Draw a picture of Jesus breaking bread and pouring wine for his disciples.

Draw a picture of people taking communion and remembering what Jesus has done for them.

Share With the Children

5'

Below are sentences for YOU to complete and share with the children. Pick one or two of them and share your own thoughts with the children. Ask the Holy Spirit and share appropriate examples or your testimonies.

- The first time I had communion was (when and where)…

- I choose to take communion because…

- When I have communion I feel…

Fun Time

Games

10+

- **"Draw it"**

  - I'm not a morning person, but on December 25th, it's a totally different story.
  - The grass is always greener on the other side of the hill.
  - Let's solve the problem together. Two heads are better than one.
  - Don't put all of your eggs in one basket. What is your backup plan?
  - Don't touch my moustache.

- **Paper Planes**

- **I Found My Dentures!**

- **The Guardian**

4.1 THE HOLY SPIRIT
HE GUIDES AND DIRECTS

Welcome   5'

Find out about the children. Share your answers first.

- Ask children what they did during the week.
- Find out children's favorite snacks, and why they like it.
- Find out where you can buy them and who buys them.

Icebreaker   Share your answers first.

- If you were to share their favorite snack with someone, who would it be and why.

Name The Books   5'

DANIEL, HOSEA
JOEL, AMOS, OBADIAH

Process

TEACHER	STUDENTS
1) Introduce the Books 2) Repeat in groups 3) Skip repetition 4) Keep the beat	Say the names of the books in the Bible by yourself and get a sticker!

Word: Lesson Objectives

It is important for children to know who the Holy Spirit is to you. Share how you have known the Holy Spirit.

The Lesson

<u>Today I would like to introduce you to the Holy Spirit.</u>
Who is the Holy Spirit?
- o   Have the children share their thoughts.

In Philippians 2:1 it says: *The Holy Spirit is our friend*
What do friends do for each other?
- o   Have the children share their thoughts.

- •   Friends help each other, encourage one another, give gifts to each other, share their hearts with each other, and comfort each other.

- •   The Holy Spirit does all of that and more for us!

Listen to the passage in Matthew 3:16-17:

> *As soon as Jesus was baptized, he came up out of the water. At that moment heaven was opened Jesus saw the Spirit of God coming down on him /Jke a dove. A voice from heaven said, "This is my Son, and I love him. I am very pleased with him. 11*

Who is speaking from heaven?

- •   God the Father is speaking from heaven.

Who is being baptized?

- •   Jesus is being baptized.

Who descended (came down) from heaven?
- o   Have the children share their thoughts.

- •   The Holy Spirit came upon Jesus and empowered Him to do the work of the Father/God.

The Holy Spirit helps us in many ways. One of the things He does is He guides us with decisions we make every day.

In Acts 8:29 it says:

> *the Spirit told Ph!lip, "Go to that chariot. Stay near it"*

InActs 16:6b it says:

> *the Holy Spirit had kept them (Paul and his companions) from preaching the word in Asia Minor.*

Do you think the Holy Spirit is guiding you also?
- Have the children share their thoughts.
- Share your thoughts.

In Galatians 5:16 it says:

> *"Live by the Holy Spirit's power. Then you will not do what your desires controlled by sin want you to do."*

What does that mean?
- Have the children share their thoughts.
- This means that we will become a person who will choose to do exactly what the Holy Spirit would choose to do.
- It means that we will not make our choices by feelings or decisions that do not come from God.

Have you ever gotten angry or jealous?
What did you do when you got angry?
- Share an appropriate story of when you got angry.
- Have the children share their stories.

Have you ever screamed, yelled, or cried?
Were those actions led by the Holy Spirit?
- Have the children share their thoughts.

What sort of actions do you think you will take when you are led by the Holy Spirit?
- Have the children share their thoughts.
- You would be kind, loving, peaceful, joyful, patient, good, faithful, gentle, and able to control yourself.
- When you desire (wish) to do good things, you are led by the Holy Spirit.
- The Holy Spirit can be saddened when we are wicked.

In Ephesians 4:30, Paul said:

> 'Do not make God's Holy Spirit mourn."

Romans 8:12-14 says:

> Brothers and sisters, we have a duty Our duty is not to live under the power of sin. If you live under the power of sin, you wt!/ die. But by the Spirit's power you can put to death the sins you commit. Then you will live. Those who are led by the Spirit of God are chtldren of God

Would you like to be led by the Holy Spirit so you can do good things?

Would you like the Holy Spirit to help you to be good every day and forever?

- ° Share your thoughts.
- ° Have the children share their desires.

Color the Picture

Activities

DRAW A PICTURE

Draw a picture of the Holy Spirit coming down on Jesus when He got baptized.

Draw a picture of the Holy Spirit leading and guiding you.

Share With the Children

5'

Below are sentences for YOU to complete and share with the children. Pick one or two of them and share your own thoughts with the children. Ask the Holy Spirit and share appropriate examples or your testimonies.

- I noticed I was not led by the Holy Spirit when...
- When the Holy Spirit is leading me I feel...
- I know Holy Spirit is a person because...

Fun Time

Games

10+

- **"Scene 1. Take 1"**

 someone blowing a trumpet, a person reading a funny book, Moses dividing the Red Sea, a person on a rollercoaster,
a lady having a cup of tea, a person digging for diamond,
a baby tasting lemon for the first time, someone playing the drums

- **Draw for the Master**

 a person drinking hot cocoa on a tree, a cat in a hat,
a fresh apple pie, a monkey on a tree with a book, the universe,
a person picking strawberries, an octopus showing eight dresses

- **The Secret Object**

- **Masking Tape Activities**

4.2 THE HOLY SPIRIT
HE IS THE TEACHER

Welcome

5'

Find out about the children. Share your answers first.

- Ask children what they did during the week.
- Find out what children do to help out their family.
- Find out what each of their families do for each other.

Icebreaker Share your answers first.

- What do you most appreciate about your parents (or a person who cares for you) and why?

Name The Books

5'

JONAH, MICAH
NAHUM, HABAKKUK

Process

TEACHER	STUDENTS
1) Introduce the Books 2) Say them like a _____ 3) Repeat in groups 4) Skip repetition	Say the names of the books in the Bible by yourself and get a sticker!

Word: Lesson Objectives

Children think adults do not have to learn or ask questions. Share with children how you ask the Holy Spirit questions and how He teaches you.

The Lesson

Last week we learned that the Holy Spirit guides and directs us.

Do you remember some stories I have shared with you?
- Have the children share any story they remember from last week.

<u>**Today we are going to learn another special thing the Holy Spirit does for us.**</u>

What do you think it could be?
- Have the children share their thoughts.

In John 14:26, this is what Jesus said:

> 'But the Father will send the Friend in my name to help you. The Friend is the Holy Spirit He w!II teach you all things. He w!II remind you of everything I have said to you. 11

According to Jesus, who sends the Holy Spirit?

- The Father sends the Holy Spirit.

What did Jesus say the Holy Spirit would do for us?

- The Holy Spirit will teach us.

Who is your friend?

- The Holy Spirit is our friend.

What is the Holy Spirit going to teach us?

- He will teach us all things.

What does the Holy Spirit help up remember?

- He helps us remember all that Jesus has said.

When you have a question about the Bible, who do you ask?
- Have the children share their thoughts.

- You ask the Holy Spirit first.

What would you like the Holy Spirit to teach you?

Are you ready to listen to Him every day?
- Have the children share their hearts.

Let's read Ephesians 5:15-18:

> So be very careful how you live. Do not live like people who aren't wise. Live like people who are wise. Make the most of every opportunity The days are evil. So don't be foolish. Instead, understand what the Lord wants. Don't fill yourself up with wine. Getting drunk will lead to wild living. Instead, be filled with the Holy Spirit.

It is very important to be filled with the Holy Spirit all the time.

What do you think being filled with the Holy Spirit means?

- ○ Have the children share their thoughts.

- • Being filled with the Holy Spirit means asking the Holy Spirit to teach us every day because we want to learn from Him.

- • It also means we are willing to listen to His voice, obey what He says, and keep doing good things.

Why do you think the Bible tells us to be filled with the Holy Spirit?

- ○ Have the children share their thoughts.

- • We need to be filled with the Holy Spirit because we are not perfect.

- • We need the Holy Spirit to help us be good and live the way God wants us to live.

How can a person be filled with the Holy Spirit?

- ○ Have the children share their thoughts.

- • We pray to Him, worship Him, listen to Him, talk to Him, and think about Him.

The Bible tells us that we can sadden the Holy Spirit. In Ephesians 4:30–31 it says:

> Do not make God's Holy Spirit mourn. The Holy Spirit is the proof that you belong to God And the Spirit is the proof that God will set you completely free. Get rid of all hard feelings, anger and rage. Stop all fighting and lying. Don't have anything to do with any kind of hatred

How can a person sadden the Holy Spirit according to these verses?

- ○ Have the children share their thoughts.

- • We can sadden the Holy Spirit when we are angry or lie or hate someone.

DRAW A PICTURE

Draw a picture of the Holy Spirit teaching you.

Draw a picture or a letter to the Holy Spirit.

Share With the Children

Below are sentences for YOU to complete and share with the children. Pick one or two of them and share your own thoughts with the children. Ask the Holy Spirit and share appropriate examples or your testimonies.

- When I asked the Holy Spirit to teach me _____ He showed me…
- When the Holy Spirit teaches me I feel…
- I ask the Holy Spirit to teach me when…

Games

Fun Time

- **"Draw it"**

  a spider, salt and light, prayer, a smile, a crib, seven bowls, a harp, an arm, oil, glass, a mirror, lake of fire, climb, a frog, a pillar of cloud, a frying pan, an electric fan, a grave, an ocean

- **Who/What am I?**

  Clothes: jeans, a red t-shirt, pajama pants, socks, a jacket, a sweater, a turtle neck sweater, a white shirt, a tie, a bow tie, gloves, a scarf, a striped shirt, a coat, boots, sandals, a hat, a cap, a skirt, a dress

- **Card Games**

- **Super Toes**

Notes

4.3 THE HOLY SPIRIT
HE GIVE THE GIFTS

Welcome	5'

Find out about the children. Share your answers first.

- Ask children what they did during the week.
- Ask children what their family do for a living.
- Find out what children would like to be when they grow up and why.

Icebreaker   Share your answers first.

- If you could wear any uniform for a day, which one would you wear and why?

Books of the Week

Name The Books	5'

S, EXODUS, LEVITICUS, NUMBERS,
DEUTERONOMY, JOSHUA, JUDGES, RUTH,
1ST & 2ND SAMUEL, 1ST & 2ND KINGS,
1ST & 2ND CHRONICLES, EZRA, NEHEMIAH, ESTHER, JOB,
PSALMS, PROVERBS, ECCLESIASTES, SONG OF SOLOMON,
ISAIAH, JEREMIAH, LAMENTATIONS, EZEKIEL, DANIEL, HOSEA,
JOEL, AMOS, OBADIAH, JONAH, MICAH, NAHU, HABAKKUK

Process

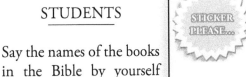

TEACHER

1) Review the Books
2) Ask for a volunteer to recite alone or with friends.
3) Encourage & reward!

STUDENTS

Say the names of the books in the Bible by yourself and get a sticker!

STICKER PLEASE...

Word: Lesson Objectives

20'

Introduce the gifts of the Holy Spirit.

The Lesson

Last week we learned that the Holy Spirit guides and directs us.
How has the Holy Spirit guided you this week?
- º First share how the Holy Spirit guided you.
- º Then encourage the children to share how the Holy Spirit guided them.

We also learned that He teaches us many things.
What did the Holy Spirit teach you this week?
- º First share what the Holy Spirit taught you.
- º Then encourage the children to share their experiences.

<u>**Today we are going to look at many different gifts the Holy Spirit gives us.**</u>
The Holy Spirit gives us gifts so we can keep following Jesus until He comes back.
Can you guess what kind of gifts they may be?
- º Have the children share their thoughts.

- • Possible answers would be the following: serving, helping, prophesying, healing, organizing, teaching, encouraging, casting out demons, telling people about Jesus, speaking in tongues, being kind to others, and so on.

Do these gifts have shapes or come in boxes?

- • **No**.

- • These are gifts we cannot see with our eyes or touch with our hands.

- • They do not have shapes or come with wrappings.

The Holy Spirit is given to each of us, and the Holy Spirit gives each of us gifts so we can help each other and help people around us in different ways.

1 Corinthians 12:7-11 says:

> *To some people the Spirit gives a message of wisdom.*
> *To others the same Spirit gives a message of knowledge. To others the same Spirit gives faith.*
> *To others that one Spirit gives gifts of healing.*
> *To others he gives the power to do miracles.*
> *To others he gives the ablfity to prophesy*
> *To others he gives the ablfity to tell the spirits apart.*
> *To others he gives the ablfity to speak in different kinds of languages they had not known before.*
> *And to still others he gives the ablfity to explain what was said in those languages.*

The Holy Spirit gives people many different kinds of gifts. This means that you and I have different gifts. Each gift helps us support and help one another.

Which one of the gifts do you think you have?
- Have the children share their thoughts.

Which one of the gifts does {your friend) have?
- Have the children share their thoughts.

Paul also teaches us that we should want the gifts of the Holy Spirit.

Which ones would you like to have?
- Have the children share which gifts they would like to have and why.
- Share with children which gifts you are asking God for.

When we learn to use the gifts of the Holy Spirit, we should be able to see some fruit produced. Paul says we should be able to tell if your gifts are of the Holy Spirit or not by the gifts' fruit.

What kind of fruit are we supposed to look for?
- Have the children share their thoughts.

Do you think they are the kind of fruit we can touch with our hands?
- Have the children share their thoughts.

- In Galatians 5:22-23 it says,

  "the fruit the Holy Spirit produces is love, joy and peace. It is being patient, kind and good It is being faithful and gentle and having control of oneself There is no law against things of that kind 11

  It is written in the book of Acts that there were many poor people in the church who needed food and money. The twelve apostles wanted to take care of all of these people but did not have time to take care of all of them because they had to share about Jesus also. So they decided to pick seven people who were wise and full of the Holy Spirit to carry out the important task. They chose Stephen, Philip, Procorus [prok'-o-rus], Nicanor [ni-ka'-nor], Timon [ti'-mon], Parmenas[par'-me-nas], and Nicolas [nik'-o-las].

What do you think these seven men were like?
- ○ Have the children share their thoughts.
- They were probably loving, joyful, gentle, patient, kind and always wanting to do good things for people.

When we see fruits like the following, we know the Holy Spirit is empowering this person to produce such fruits.
- ○ Have the children complete the following sentences with their own words.
  When you have

love, you will... (think that other person's happiness is more important.)

joy, you will... (give great happiness to someone.)

peace, you feel... (calm and not worries.)

patience, you will... (stay calm and not get annoyed when something takes a long time.)

kindness, you will... (be gentle, caring and helpful to others.)

goodness, you will... (be kind, helpful and honest.) faithfulness, you will... (keep your promises.)

gentleness, you will... (be caring, tender, and calm.)

self-control, you are able to... (control your feelings.)

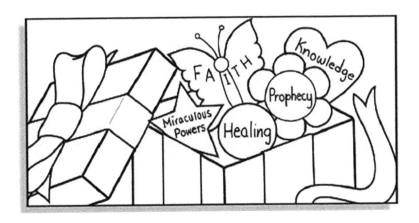

5'

DRAW A PICTURE

Draw a picture of yourself receiving the gifts of the Holy Spirit.

Draw a picture of the fruits of the Holy Spirit.

Share With the Children

5'

Below are sentences for YOU to complete and share with the children. Pick one or two of them and share your own thoughts with the children. Ask the Holy Spirit and share appropriate examples or your testimonies.

- I think the Holy Spirit has given me a gift of _____ because...
- The first time I saw a person healed by the gift of healing was...
- I know a person who has gift of hospitality. (describe)

Games

10+

Fun Time

- **Telephone**
    - A picture is worth a thousand words.
    - It is better to give than to receive. Be a cheerful giver.
    - Genius is one percent inspiration, ninety-nine percent perspiration.
    - God will bring us to where we really want to be.

- **Paper Planes**

- **I Found My Dentures!**

- **Mission Balance**

5.1 TALKING AND LISTENING
HOW IT WORKS

| Welcome | 5' |

Find out about the children. Share your answers first.

- Ask children what they did during the week.
- Find out what children's favorite colors are and why.
- Find out what colors they would like to paint their houses.

Icebreaker Share your answers first.

If you could paint anything with your favorite color, what object would you paint with that color?

Books of the Week

| Name The Books | 5' |

ZEPHANIAH

HAGGAI

ZECHARIAH

MALACHI

Process

TEACHER
1) Introduce the Books
2) Repeat in groups
3) Skip repetition
4) Keep the beat

STUDENTS
Say the names of the books in the Bible by yourself and get a sticker!

STICKER PLEASE...

Share with children how you listen to God. Help them understand that when you listen to God you are not talking, just listening.

The Lesson

Today we are going to learn about listening to God's voice.

Listen to this story carefully. In John 10:2-5 it says:

> *The one who enters through the gate is the shepherd of the sheep. The gatekeeper opens the gate for him. The sheep listen to his voice. He calls his own sheep by name and leads them out. When he has brought all of hisown sheep out, he goes on ahead of them. His sheep follow him because they know his voice. But they will never follow a stranger. In fact, they will run away from him. They don't recognize a stranger's voice.*

Who calls the sheep?

  ◦   Have the children share their thoughts.

  •   The shepherd calls the sheep.

Who is the shepherd?

  ◦   Have the children share their thoughts.

  •   Jesus is the shepherd.

How does the shepherd call his sheep?

  ◦   Have the children share their thoughts.

  •   He calls them by their name.

Do sheep listen to the shepherd?

  •   Yes, they do.

What do sheep do when they hear their shepherd's voice?

  •   They follow him.

Why do you think sheep follow the voice of the shepherd?

  ◦   Have the children share their thoughts.

  •   Sheep know the shepherd's voice, and they trust him.

  •   Jesus said we are like sheep, and He is the Shepherd.

Does God know your name?

  •   Yes.

Does Jesus know your name?

  •   Yes.

The Lesson

Have you ever heard God call your name?
- ○ Have the children share their experiences.
- ○ Share an appropriate example of your hearing God's voice.

Let's close our eyes and listen to Him call our names.
- ○ Take a moment to listen to God.
- ○ Ask children if they heard Him call their names.

Let's think about how listening and talking work.

Are you able to listen to your friends if you talk when they are talking?
- ○ Have the children share their thoughts.

- • No, we cannot listen and talk at the same time.

Do you think your friends are listening to you if they talk when you are talking?
- ○ Have the children share their thoughts.

- • No, we do not feel we are being heard if another person talks when we are talking.

Let's do an experiment.
- ○ Have the children talk to each other at the same time. (Example: say their name, birthday, favorite color, and so on.)

Were you able to understand each other well?
- ○ Have the children share their thoughts.

- • We can not talk and listen at the same time.

- • When someone is talking you have to listen.

- • When you pay attention and listen to someone, you will hear and understand what the person is saying.

Listening is a very important skill to learn. When you listen to someone, you pay your full attention to that person. When God is speaking to you, you need to pay your full attention to God and listen to His voice.

Why is it important to listen to God's voice?
- ○ Have the children share their thoughts.

- • It is important to know God's voice because there are many other voices that may try to make us do bad things or lead us to believe wrong things.

DRAW A PICTURE

Draw a picture of a sheep listening to the shepherd's voice.

Draw a picture of your friend talking and you listening to your friend.

Below are sentences for YOU to complete and share with the children. Pick one or two of them and share your own thoughts with the children. Ask the Holy Spirit and share appropriate examples or your testimonies.

- The first time I recognized the voice of Jesus was… (explain).

- When I did not know His voice I was _____ but when I learned to follow His voice I…

- I know a person who learned to follow His voice and (explain what happened).

Games

10+

- **"Scene 1. Take 1"**

 a person cracking eggs, someone being baptized, a dog swimming, an elephant swimming, a turtle eating popcorn, a tennis game,
a person drinking a glass of milk, someone eating a banana

- **Draw for the Master**

 a bird on a swing, a banana under a table, a bee on a boat,
a frog jumping on a log, a cat taking a nap, a person on a skateboard, an apple on top of an orange, a happy fish

- **The Secret Object**

- **Paper Dash**

Notes

5.2 TALKING AND LISTENING
SAMUEL'S CASE

Welcome   5'

Find out about the children. Share your answers first.

- Ask children what they did during the week.
- Find out who children's heroes are and why they consider them heroes.
- Ask children if they know a person who is like the super hero they mentioned.

Icebreaker   Share your answers first.

- If you could meet anyone in the world, who would you like to meet, and why would you like to meet him or her?

Books of the Week

Name The Books   5'

IS, EXODUS, LEVITICUS NUMBERS,
DEUTERONOMY, JOSHUA, JUDGES, RUTH,
1ST & 2ND SAMUEL, 1ST & 2ND KINGS,
1ST & 2ND CHRONICLES, EZRA, NEHEMIAH, ESTHER, JOB,
PSALMS, PROVERBS, ECCLESIASTES, SONG OF SOLOMON,
ISAIAH, JEREMIAH, LAMENTATIONS, EZEKIEL, DANIEL,
HOSEA, JOEL, AMOS, OBADIAH, JONAH, MICAH, NAHUM,
HABAKKUK, ZEPHANIAH, HAGGAI, ZECHARIAH, MALACHI

Process

TEACHER	STUDENTS
1) Review the Books 2) Ask for a volunteer to recite alone or with friends. 3) Encourage & reward!	Say the names of the books in the Bible by yourself and get a sticker!

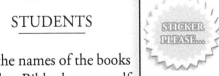

STICKER PLEASE...

Word: Lesson Objectives

20'

Help children understand how Samuel learned to listen to God's voice.
The activity in this lesson is long. Complete this lesson in two weeks if necessary.

The Lesson

Last week we learned that we need to listen to learn God's voice.
Today we will learn how Samuel learned to listen to God's voice.
Listen to the story of Samuel.

> Samuel was born to Elkanah (his father) and Hannah (his mother). Samuel's mother, Hannah, prayed to God in the Temple for a son, because she did not have children. She told God that if God gave her a son, she would give the child back to God. God answered her prayer and gave her a son, and she named him Samuel. When Samuel stopped nursing, his mom, Hannah, brought him to the Temple of the LORD just as she had promised to God. So Samuel grew up in the Temple of the LORD, serving Eli, the priest.
>
> As Samuel grew up, he learned to hear God speak to him and everything Samuel heard from God came true. So all the people of Israel recognized that Samuel really was a prophet of the _LORD_.

Do you think Samuel learned to listen to God right away?
  o   Have the children share their thoughts.

Open your Splash Zone Children's Activity Book to Unit 5 Lesson 2
<u>Listen to the story of Samuel and draw a picture of the scene in Box 1.</u>
1 Samuel 3:1b–2:

> _In those days the Lord didn't give many messages to his people. He didn't give them any visions. One night Eli was lying down in his usual place. His eyes were becoming so weak he couldn't see very well._

  o   Have the children draw a picture of this scene in Box 1.

<u>Listen to the next part of the story and draw a picture of the scene in Box 2.</u>
1 Samuel 3:3–4:

> _Samuel was lying down in the Lord's house. That's where the ark of God was kept. The lamp of God was still burning. The Lord called out to Samuel. Samu el answered, "Here I am."_

  o   Have the children draw a picture of this scene in Box 2.

The Lesson

Listen to the next part of the story and draw a picture of the scene in Box 3.

1 Samuel 3:5a:

> *He ran over to Eli and said, "Here I am. You called out to me."*

Who called Samuel?

- God called Samuel.

Who did Samuel think called him?

- Samuel thought Eli called him.
- Have the children draw a picture of this scene in Box 3.

Listen to the next part of the story and draw a picture of the scene in Box 4.

1 Samuel 3:5b:

> *But Eli said, 'I didn't call you. Go back and lie down." So he went and lay down.*

Did Eli call Samuel?

- No, Eli did not call Samuel.

What did Eli tell Samuel to do?

- Eli told Samuel to go back to bed because he did not call him.
- Have the children draw a picture of this scene in Box 4.

Listen to the next part of the story and draw a picture of the scene in Box 5.

1 Samuel 3:6:

> *Again the Lord called out, "Samuel!" Samuel got up and went to Eli He said, "Here I am. You called out to me." "My son" Eli said, 'I didn't call you. Go back and lie down."*

Who called Samuel?

- God called Samuel.

Who did Samuel think called him?

- Samuel thought Eli called him.

What did Eli tell Samuel to do?

- Eli told Samuel to go back to bed because he did not call him.
- Have the children draw a picture of this scene in Box 5.

Listen to the next part of the story and draw a picture of the scene in Box 6.

> God called Samuel for the third time, and that's when it dawned on Eli that God was calling the boy. *So Eli told Samuel, "Go and lie down. If someone calls out to you again, say, 'Speak, Lord I'm listening.'"* (1 Samuel 3:9)

Who did Eli think was calling Samuel?

- Eli thought it was God calling Samuel.

What did Eli tell Samuel to do this time?

- Eli told Samuel to say, "Speak, Lord. I am listening."
- Have the children draw a picture of this scene in Box 6.

Listen to the next part of the story and draw a picture of the scene in Box 7.
1 Samuel 3:10a:

> *The Lord came and stood there. He called out just as he had done the other times. He said, "Samuel! Samuel!"*

Who called Samuel?

- God called Samuel.

Where was God?

- He came to Samuel's room and stood there.

Who did Samuel think called him?

- This time Samuel knew it was God who had called him.
- Have the children draw a picture of this scene in Box 7.

Listen to the next part of the story and draw a picture of the scene in Box 8.
1 Samuel 3:10b:

> *Then Samuel replied, "Speak. I'm listening."*

- Have the children draw a picture of this scene in Box 8.

Let's share what we have drawn and tell Samuel's story with your cartoon.

Draw a Cartoon

Eli was lying down in his room. Samuel was in bed in the Temple of God.

The Lord called out Samuel. Samuel answered, "Here I am."

This happened two more times!

This third time, Eli knew God was calling Samuel, so he said, "If the voice calls again, say, 'Speak God. I am listening.'"

Samuel ran over to Eli and said, "Here I am. You called out to me."

But Eli said, "I did not call you. Go back and lay down." Samuel did.

Samuel went and laid down in his place. The Lord came and stood there. He said, "Samuel!"

Then Samuel replied, "Speak God. I am listening."

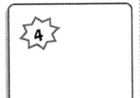

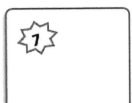

1 Samuel 3:1–10 (NIRV)

Below are sentences for YOU to complete and share with the children. Pick one or two of them and share your own thoughts with the children. Ask the Holy Spirit and share appropriate examples or your testimonies.

- The first time I followed God's voice was… (explain)

- To me God's voice sounds like… (share your experience).

- When I am not sure if it I am hearing from God or not I…

Fun Time

Games

10+

- **"Draw it"**

 world, valley, father, anchor, burnt offering, drink, an open door, a gong, a bucket, a shepherd, an apple, earrings, hair, hay, lion's den, meat, mouth, seeds, song, nose

- **Who/What am I?**

 Kitchen item: a refrigerator, an oven, faucet, a plate, a spoon, a fork, a blender, a pot, a frying pan, a ladle, a mug, a mug, a bowl, a glass, a spatula, a toaster oven, a water pitcher

- **Card Games**

- **Super Toes**

5.3 TALKING AND LISTENING
HOW JESUS LISTENED

Welcome
5'

Find out about the children. Share your answers first.
- What was the best thing that happened this week?
- Find out children's favorite instrument and why they like the instrument.
- Find out if children play any musical instruments.

Icebreaker   Share your answers first.
- If you could play any instrument, what would it be and why?

Books of the Week

Name The Books
5'

IS, EXODUS, LEVITICUS NUMBERS,
DEUTERONOMY, JOSHUA, JUDGES, RUTH,
1ST & 2ND SAMUEL, 1ST & 2ND KINGS,
1ST & 2ND CHRONICLES, EZRA, NEHEMIAH, ESTHER, JOB,
PSALMS, PROVERBS, ECCLESIASTES, SONG OF SOLOMON,
ISAIAH, JEREMIAH, LAMENTATIONS, EZEKIEL, DANIEL,
HOSEA, JOEL, AMOS, OBADIAH, JONAH, MICAH, NAHUM,
HABAKKUK, ZEPHANIAH, HAGGAI, ZECHARIAH, MALACHI

Process

TEACHER	STUDENTS
1) Ask for a volunteer to recite alone or with friends. 2) Take a video 3) Encourage & reward!	Say the names of the books in the Bible by yourself and get a sticker!

STICKER PLEASE...

Word: Lesson Objectives

Share with children how Jesus took his time to listen to God's voice.
It is important to share with the children how you take your time to listen to God.

The Lesson

Today we are going to learn how Jesus talked and listened to God.

Prayer is talking to God. There are verses in the Bible that shows us how Jesus spent time talking with God.

Luke 5:15-16 says:

> But the news about Jesus spread further. So crowds of people came to hear him. They also came to be healed of their sicknesses. But Jesus often went away to be by himself and pray

What is happening to Jesus in this scene?

- o   Have the children share their answers.

- •   People heard about Jesus and came to Him to hear Him or to be healed.

Where did Jesus go to pray/talk to God?

- o   Have the children share their answers.

- •   He went away to be by Himself and pray (spend time with God).

Mark 1:35 says:

> It was very early in the morning and still dark Jesus got up and left the house. He went to a place where he could be alone. There he prayed

Where did Jesus go?

- o   Have the children share their answers.

- •   He went to a place where He could be alone.

What did he do there?

- o   Have the children share their answers.

- •   He prayed (spent time with God).

- •   Jesus spent time talking to His Father and listened to Him.

What time of the day did Jesus spend time with God?

- o   Have the children share their thoughts.

- •   It was very early in the morning and still dark. It was during the fourth watch of the night, from three o'clock in the morning until six o'clock, approximately.

Why do you think Jesus woke up early in the morning to pray?

- o   Have the children share their thoughts.

- •   It is very quiet in the morning when it is still dark.

Have you ever tried to be alone? If so, where were you?
- ○ Share your own experience.
- ○ Have the children share their experiences.

Do you remember how you felt when you were alone?
- ○ Share how you felt.
- ○ Have the children share how they felt.

Why do you think Jesus chose to be alone when He prayed {spent time with God)?
- ○ Have the children share their thoughts.

- • He showed us an example because we might need to go to a quiet place to talk with God and listen to Him. We get distracted very easily.

How many times did He spend time with God by Himself?
- ○ Have the children share their guesses.

- • He spent time with God by Himself a lot.

Here is another example.

> On one of those days, Jesus went out to a mountainside to pray He spent the night praying to GodrLuke 6·12).

Where did Jesus go to spend time with God?
- ○ Have the children share their answers.

- • He went out to a mountainside.

Why do you think he went to the mountainside?
- ○ Have the children share their thoughts.

- • He went to the mountainside to be alone with God.

What time of the day did Jesus spend time with God?
- ○ Have the children share their thoughts.

- • He spent the night praying.

- • He also prayed early in the morning.

Do you think Jesus thought it was important to spend time talking and listening to His Father, God? Why?
- ° Have the children share their thoughts.
- ° Share with children how you spend time with God.

- • You can talk and listen to God anywhere, but Jesus set aside a special time and place to spend time with God.

Where would your quiet place be?
- ° Have the children share their answers.
- ° Help the children find a place.

- • Places might include space in a closet, under a table, in the shower, behind furniture, behind a curtain, in the back yard.

When would be the best time for you go there and talk to God?
- ° Have the children share their answers.
- ° Help children identify times of the day to be with God.

- • Times might include time in the morning, time before going to bed, shower time, time spent walking to school, or time in the car.

Color the Picture

Activities

5'

DRAW A PICTURE

Draw a special place where you and Jesus talk to each other.

Share With the Children

Below are sentences for YOU to complete and share with the children. Pick one or two of them and share your own thoughts with the children. Ask the Holy Spirit and share appropriate examples or your testimonies.

- I spend my time alone with God (share with the children where you spend time with God.)

- I like to listen to God and talk with Him there because…

- When I don't spend much time with Him I feel…

Fun Time

Games

- **Telephone**

  - That's one small step for a man, a giant step for mankind.
  - A penny saved is a penny earned.
  - Actions speak louder than words.
  - Learning is a treasure that will follow it's owner everywhere.
  - Let another person praise you, and not your own mouth. Proverbs 27:2

- **Paper Planes**

- **I Found My Dentures!**

- **The Guardian**

Welcome

Find out about the children. Share your answers first.

- Ask children what they did during the week,
- Find out children's favorite foods and why they like them.
- Find out what is the best thing children have ever eaten.

Icebreaker Share your answers first.

- If you were to share your favorite food with someone, who would it be and why?

Books of the Week

Name The Books

MATTHEW

MARK

LUKE

JOHN

Process

TEACHER	STUDENTS
1) Introduce the Books 2) Repeat in groups 3) Skip repetition 4) Keep the beat	Say the names of the books in the Bible by yourself and get a sticker!

STICKER PLEASE...

Help children understand what it means to have faith in God. Share an appropriate story of how God built your faith.

The Lesson

Today we are going to talk about faith.
What is faith?
- ° Have the children share their thoughts.
- • Faith means I believe something even if I cannot see it.
- • We see that "something" with the eyes of our hearts.

When someone says Jimmy has "faith in God," what do you think it means?
- ° Have the children share their thoughts.
- • It means Jimmy believes in God even when he cannot see God.

Did you know that God made eyes for your heart too?
- • Faith is the ability you use the eyes of our hearts to see the things we cannot see with the eyes of our head.
- • • We have faith when we believe there is a God.

Can we see God?
- ° Have the children share their thoughts.
- • No, we cannot see God with our physical eyes.
- • We know He is real because we see Him with the eyes of our hearts, and we have faith.

Hebrews 11:6 says:

> *And without faith it is impossible to please God, because anyone who comes to him must believe that he exists and that he rewards those who earnestly seek him.*

Do you know any person in the Bible that had strong faith in God?
- ° Have the children share what they know.

Listen to the story of Abraham.

> *There was a man named Abraham who loved God. God loved Abraham too.*
>
> *When Abraham was one hundred years old, his wife Sarah had a child and he named his son Isaac. Abraham loved Isaac so much that God wanted to see if Abraham loved his son Isaac more than he loved God. He told Abraham to go to Moriah and offer Isaac as a burnt offering.*
>
> *The next morning Abraham got up early, put a saddle on his donkey, and set out on a journey with Isaac. He brought two of his servants along to carry wood for the burnt offering. Three days later, they saw the place in the distance. Abraham told the servants to stay there. Abraham brought the fire and the knife, placed the wood on Isaac to carry, and started out for the place where God had told him to go.*

Genesis 22:6–8 says Abraham and Isaac had a conversation like this:

> *Isaac said to his father, Abraham, "Father?" "Yes, my son?" Abraham replied "The fire and wood are here, 11 Isaac said "But where is the lamb for the burnt offering?" Abraham answered, "God himself will provide the lamb for the burnt offering, my son. 11 The two of them walked on together.*

Did Abraham or Isaac see the lamb for the sacrifice?

- No, they did not.

Why do you think Abraham and Isaac kept climbing the mountain even when they did not see the lamb to sacrifice?

- ○ Have the children share their thoughts.

- Abraham had faith in God.

- Abraham believed even if God did not provide the lamb he knew God could raise his son from the dead.

Let's continue on with the story.

> *When Abraham and Isaac reached the place God had told them to go, Abraham built an altar. An altar is a place where you put sacrifices. Sacrifice is something you give up. Abraham placed the wood on the altar, tied up Isaac, and put him on top of the wood. Then he took the knife to kill his son*

The Lesson

Did Abraham decide to disobey God because he would have to offer Isaac?

- No, he didn't.

Why do you think Abraham did not stop?

○ Have the children share their thoughts.

- Abraham had faith in God.

- Abraham was willing to obey God because he knew that God loved him and was faithful to him.

What is going to happen next? Let's continue on with the story.
Genesis 22:11-13 says:

> the angel of the LORD called out to him from heaven. He said, "Abraham! Abraham!" "Here I am, "Abraham replied "Do not lay a hand on the boy," he said "Do not harm him. Now I know that you would do anything for God You have not held back from me your son, your only son. 11 Abraham looked around There in a bush he saw a ram caught by its horns. He went over and took the ram. He sacrificed it as a burnt offering instead of his son.

What did God do for Abraham and Isaac?

○ Have the children share their answers.

- God provided a ram so Abraham can offer the ram instead of Isaac.

- God saw their faith and provided a way out for them.

- Abraham named that place The Lord Will Provide. (v.14)

Listen to the rest of the story and see what happened as a result of their faith.

> Then Abraham heard the angel call out from heaven again. The Angle made an announcement that God is going to protect Abraham and be kind to him because he was willing to give his only son to Him.

> God said that He will multiply children born into Abraham's family and they will be so many like the stars in the sky, and the sand on the seashore. God also told Abraham, "All nations on earth will be blessed because of your children. All these things will happen because you have obeyed me." (v.18)

What happened as a result of Abraham's faith in God?

○ Have the children share their answers.

- God accepted Abraham and his faith made him right with God.

- God blessed Abraham with many, many, children.

- Everyone on earth will be blessed as a result of his faith.

DRAW A PICTURE

Draw a picture of the story you heard today. Tell the story to your friends.

Share With the Children

Below are sentences for YOU to complete and share with the children. Pick one or two of them and share your own thoughts with the children. Ask the Holy Spirit and share appropriate examples or your testimonies.

- If I had not put my trust in God, I probably would have…
  (Share an appropriate story.)

- Reading the Bible helps build up my faith because…

- My favorite story in the Bible about faith is…

Games

- **"Scene 1. Take 1"**

   a man shaving his mustache, someone sewing, a person baking a cake, someone skipping with an ice cream cone, someone making a sandwich, a person looking for a pearl in the mud,

- **Draw for the Master**

   a person taking a picture of his dog, a girl eating lemon in a box,
  a cat taking a nap on a polka-dot blanket, a vase on a table,
  an angel protecting a person from a car accident,
  a person sleeping on a tree

- **The Secret Object**

- **Masking Tape Activities**

6.2 MORE LISTENING
DREAMS

Welcome 5'

Find out about the children. Share your answers first.

- Ask children what they did during the week,
- Find out what children's favorite movies are and why.
- Find our where they saw the movie and who they saw the movie with.

Icebreaker   Share your answers first.

- If you could invite one person from a movie to be a part of your family, who would it be and why?

Books of the Week

Name The Books 5'

ACTS
ROMANS
1ST & 2ND CORINTHIANS

Process

TEACHER	STUDENTS
1) Introduce the Books 2) Say them like a _____ 3) Repeat groups 4) Skip repetition	Say the names of the books in the Bible by yourself and get a sticker!

STICKER PLEASE...

Share with the children that God speaks to us through dreams. Pray for children who have nightmares. Ask God to give them His dreams.

The Lesson

<u>**Today we will talk about how God speaks through dreams.**</u>
Have you ever had dreams?
- o o Have the children share their dreams.

Did you know that God speaks through dreams, too?
- o o Have the children share their thoughts.

There is a story of a person named Jacob who had a dream from God.

> Jacob had a brother named Esau. One day he tricked his brother Esau and his father Isaac, to take the blessings his brother had. Jacob ran away from his brother and went on a long journey by himself to go to his uncle's place in Haran. When he stopped to sleep, he looked for a stone to put under his head for a pillow.

Jacob was traveling in the desert alone. Were there any lights at nighttime?
- o Have the children share their thoughts.

- • No. It was very dark with only the moonlight and stars to guide him.

How do you think Jacob must have felt traveling in the dark?
- o Have the children share their thoughts.

- • He must have been very lonely and scared while walking alone.

> When Jacob used the stone as a pillow, he had a dream. In his dream he saw a stairway going all the way up to heaven from the ground.

Can you guess who were going up and down the stairway?
- o Have the children share their guesses.

- • God's Angels were going were going up and down the stairs.

Can you guess who was by the stairway?
- o Have the children share their guesses.

Listen to Genesis 28:13-15 and find out.

Genesis 28:13-15 says:

> the LORD stood beside the stairway He said, 'Jam the LORD. I am the God of your grandfather Abraham and the God of Isaac. I wdl give you and your children after you the land you are lying on. They will be like the dust of the earth that can't be counted They will spread out to the west and to the east. They will spread out to the north and to the south. All nations on earth will be blessed because of you and your children after you. I am with you. I will watch over you everywhere you go. And I will bring you back to this land I will not leave you unfll I have done what I have promised you."

What did God show Jacob through his dream?

- ○ Have the children share their thoughts.

- • God showed Jacob that He would never leave him.

- • The dream was about God's promise to Jacob.

How do you think Jacob felt after he had this dream?
Do you think he was lonely and afraid after he had this dream?

- ○ Share your answers first.
- ○ Have the children share their thoughts.
- • He probably felt comforted and encouraged.

Let's continue with Jacob's story from Genesis 28.

> Jacob woke up and realized that the dream he had was from God. When morning came, he decided to set the stone he used for a pillow to remember the exact place he had the dream. He named the place Bethel.

In Genesis 37, there is another story of a dream that a man named Joseph had.

> Joseph had eleven older brothers. When Joseph was a teenager, God started to give Joseph dreams. Two of the dreams made his family jealous and angry toward him, because the dreams said that one day his family would come to him and bow down to him. Many years later, his dreams did come true, but Joseph got in trouble for sharing these dreams with pride. Later In his life, God gave Joseph the ability to interpret dreams.

Joseph interpreted dreams. Interpret means to explain, decode, or translate.

Have you ever had dreams?
- Have the children share the dreams they had.
- Do not focus on negative or scary dreams.

- Many dreams come in symbols.

- When your dream does not make sense, it probably needs to be interpreted.

- Joseph interpreted dreams for other people including Pharaoh and became a leader of Egypt.

Would you like to be able to interpret dreams?
- Have the children share their thoughts.

Do you remember all of your dreams?
- Have the children share their experiences.

In the book of Job, it says God speaks in dreams and we may not remember them.

Job 33:14-15 says:

> Job was suffering from ternble tllness and complaining that God was not speaking to him. His friend, Elihu, told Job, "Job, don't say God is not speaking to you! God speaks in dreams when you are asleep and you may not even remember it!"

God gives us dreams to speak to us but there are dreams that are not from God.

How can you tell if your dream is from God or not?
- Have the children share their thoughts.

- We can find out if the dream is from God by asking Him if the dream was from Him.

- We can ask our parents if they think our dreams were from God or not.

- We can also test our dreams with the Bible by seeing if the messages of the dreams line up with the Bible.

Color the Picture

Activities

DRAW A PICTURE

Draw a picture of Jacob's dream or Joseph's dream.

Draw a picture of one of the happiest dreams you had or ask God for a picture and draw what you see.

Share With the Children

Below are sentences for YOU to complete and share with the children. Pick one or two of them and share your own thoughts with the children. Ask the Holy Spirit and share appropriate examples or your testimonies.

- The most amazing/exciting/beautiful dream I had was...

- When I have dreams I do not understand I... (share what you do).

- When I have scary dreams I... (explain what you do).

- My favorite dream story in the Bible is...

Fun Time

Games

- **"Draw it"**

 leaf, footprint, a whip, lamb, honey, a fly, a pocket, a scepter, queen, hail, money, water, sparks, herbs, a pen, a treasure chest, stop, a star, curtains, a turkey

- **Draw for the Master**

 Vehicles: air plane, helicopter, motor cycle, automobile, trucks, bus, taxi, bicycle, unicycle, tricycle, row boat, ship, train, submarine, space ship, yacht

- **Card Games**

- **Super Toes**

6.3 MORE LISTENING
PROPHECY

Welcome — 5'

Find out about the children. Share your answers first.

- Ask children what they did during the week,
- Find out the most difficult thing children have done.
- Ask how they felt when they were doing it.

Icebreaker   Share your answers first.

- Who is the strongest person you know, and how do you know he or she is strong?

Books of the Week

Name The Books — 5'

MATTHEW, MARK
LUKE, JOHN,
ACTS, ROMANS,
1ST & 2ND CORINTHIANS

Process

TEACHER	STUDENTS
1) Ask for a volunteer to recite alone or with friends. 2) Take a video 3) Encourage & reward!	Say the names of the books in the Bible by yourself and get a sticker!

STICKER PLEASE...

Word: Lesson Objectives

Help children be familiar with prophecy.

The Lesson

<u>**Today we are going to talk about prophecy.**</u>
What is prophecy?
Can you share what you think it might be?
   ○   Have the children share their thoughts.

   •   Prophecy is a message from God.
Why do you think prophetic work is important?
   ○   Have the children share their thoughts.

   •   Prophetic word from God is important because:
1. Prophetic words feed us and give us courage and strength to do what God wants us to do.
2. Prophecy helps us become who God created us to be.
Do you remember the story of Samuel?
   ○   Have the children share what they remember about Samuel.

   Samuel learned to hear the voice of God at a young age and became a prophet. When Samuel became an adult, he prophesied that Saul would become the king of Israel.

There was a king named Saul in Israel. This is how Saul became the king of Israel through prophecy (1 Samuel 9-11).

   Saul's father had many donkeys. One day some of his donkeys wandered away and were lost. He told Saul to look for the donkeys with one of his servants. They traveled quite a bit but couldn't find the donkeys, and they were lost. The servant remembered that they were in the area where the prophet Samuel lived. He thought Samuel, the prophet, could show them the way home, so they went to see him. When Saul reached Samuel, Samuel al ready knew that Saul was coming and who Saul was.

Why do you think Samuel knew that Saul was coming to see him?
   ○   Have the children share their thoughts.

   •   Samuel knew ahead of time that Saul was coming, because God had told him.

   •   God gave Samuel a prophetic word.

1 Samuel 9:16a says:

> *The day before Saul came, God spoke to Samuel and said,*
> *"About this time tomorrow I will send you a man. He is from the land of Benjamin."*

How do you feel about God telling you what it is about to take place?

- ○ Have the children share how they feel.
- ○ Share how you feel.

God also gave Samuel an instruction and told him His plan for Saul the day before he met Saul. 1 Samuel 9:16b-17 says:

> *God said, "Anoint him (Saul) to be the leader of my people Israel. He will save them from the powerful hand of the Phtlistines. I have seen how much my people are suffering. Their cry for help has reached me." When Samuel saw a man coming toward him, the LORD spoke to Samuel again. He said, "He is the man I told you about His name is Saul He wt!/ govern my people."*

How did Samuel find out that the man who was walking toward him was the one he was supposed to meet?

- • God told him.

How did Samuel find out that the man's name was Saul?

- • God told him.

Why did Samuel know that Saul was going to be the king of Israel?

- • God told him.

    When Saul approached Samuel, he told him not to worry about the donkeys he was looking for, because they had already been found.

Why did Samuel know that the donkeys were already found?

- • God told him.

    Samuel had set up a surprise dinner for Saul. He invited thirty people ahead of time an set aside a special steak dinner just for him.

1 Samuel 10:1 says:

> *(The next day) Samuel poured oil over Saul and anointed him. Samuel told Saul that God had chosen him to be king over Israel*

How do you think Saul might have felt?

- Have the children share their thoughts.

Do you think he was able to believe him right away?

○ Have the children share their thoughts.

- No, Saul didn't think he came from an important family or had a destiny to do anything great. He did not believe Samuel's word was true.

Samuel gave other prophetic words to Saul.
1 Samuel 10:2-4 says:

> *When you (Saul) leave me (Samuel) today, you will meet two men. They will be near Rachel's tomb at Zelzah on the border of Benjamin. They'll say to you, 'The donkeys you have been looking for have been found Now your father has stopped thinking about them. Instead, he's worried about you. He's asking, "What can I do to find my son?"'*

> *"You will go on from Zelzah until you come to the large tree at Tabor. Three men will meet you there. They'll be on their way up to Bethel to worship God One of them will be carrying three young goats. Another will be carrying three loaves of bread A third will be carrying a bottle of wine. It will be a bottle made out of animal skin. The men will greet you. They'll offer you two loaves of bread You will accept the loaves from them." All of this took place on his way home.*

What do you think Saul might have felt when everything that Samuel had told him came true?

○ Have the children share their thoughts.

- The prophetic word coming true must have helped Saul believe that He was chosen by God to be the king.

All of those things happened and Saul was chosen to be the king.

Do you think God gives prophetic words for us too?

- ○ Have the children share their thoughts.

- • Yes, He does.

Why do you think God wants us to listen to prophetic words?

- ○ Have the children share their thoughts.

- • God wants us to listen to His prophetic words because He wants us to find out who we really are just like Saul found how God saw him.

- • He also wants us to see what He sees us doing.

Do you think God is excited to tell us things that will take place in the future?

- ○ Have the children share their thoughts.

- • Yes, He is.

If you have received a prophetic word from God, what should you do?

- ○ Have the children share their thoughts.

- • You should go to your parents and share what God has told you.

- • Pray with your parents and ask God what to do with the word you have received.

- • See if the word you have received matches with what the Bible says.

DRAW A PICTURE

Draw a picture of God telling Samuel that Saul was coming to his place.

Draw a picture of God giving you a prophetic word.

Below are sentences for YOU to complete and share with the children. Pick one or two of them and share your own thoughts with the children. Ask the Holy Spirit and share appropriate examples or your testimonies.

- When I received a prophetic word from someone, I felt…

- When I listened to God and shared (a prophetic word), the person…

- My favorite story related with prophecy in the Bible is…

Games

- **"Draw it"**

  - The right word at the right time is like golden apples in silver jewelry. Proverbs 25:11
  - A watched pot never boils.
  - God gave us one tongue and two ears so we could hear twice as much as we speak.
  - Strong people stand for themselves but stronger people stand for others.
  - Eat an apple on going to bed, and you'll keep the doctor from earning his bread.

- **Paper Planes**

- **I Found My Dentures!**

- **Mission Balance**

Notes

7.1 MAKING GOOD CHOICES
CHOOSING TO "APOLOGIZE"

Welcome
5'

Find out about the children. Share your answers first.

- Ask children what they did during the week.
- Find out what board games the children like to play and why.
- Ask children what kinds of board games they would like to create.

Icebreaker   Share your answers first.

- If you could make one rule in your home, what would it be and why?

Books of the Week

Name The Books
5'

GALATIANS
EPHESIANS
PHILIPPIANS
COLOSSIANS

Process

TEACHER	STUDENTS
1) Introduce the Books 2) Repeat in groups 3) Skip repetition $) Keep the beat	Say the names of the books in the Bible by yourself and get a sticker!

Word: Lesson Objectives

Help the children understand that apologizing is a choice we make.
Children believe that adults never sin and do not need to apologize. Share how you also have needed to apologize.

The good choice we are going to talk about is apologizing.
Have you ever apologized?
- ° Share an appropriate story of an occasion when you needed to apologize.
- ° Have the children share their situations.

Do you find it hard to apologize, or is it easy?
- ° Have the children share if apologizing is easy for them or not.
- ° Share your thoughts.

Why do you think it is difficult/easy to apologize?
- ° Have the children share their experiences.
- ° Share an appropriate story of an occasion when you found it hard or easy to apologize.

- • Apologizing can be a very difficult thing to do.

One thing that keeps us from apologizing is pride. When you have pride, you do not want to apologize because you do not want people to think that you have made a mis take or that you have hurt someone. Our pride can get in the way of apologizing.

Answer yes or no.

Pride makes you feel like you are a loser if you apologize. (Yes)
Pride says, "I am not a bad person, and I do everything right." (Yes)
Pride says "Do not let anyone think that you have made a mistake." (Yes)

Apologizing does completely the opposite of pride.

- • When you choose to apologize, you are saying that you try to do things right.

- • When you choose to apologize, you are saying you are willing to change so that you can be a better person.

- • When you choose to apologize, you become very powerful.

- • When you choose to apologize, you become a winner.

In Genesis 50, there is a story about Joseph.

What was the dream Joseph had about him and his brothers?
- Have the children share their answers.
- Go back to Unit 6, Lesson 2, if necessary.

> Joseph thought he was better than his brothers because he had a dream from God. The dream said that someday Joseph's brothers were going to bow down to him. Joseph got big headed and told his brothers about his dream with pride. His brothers got so jealous that they threw Joseph into a pit and then sold him to the Ishmaelites.

Do you think throwing Joseph into a pit and selling him was the right thing to do, because Joseph was prideful? Why do you think so?
- Have the children share their thoughts.
- No, they should not have done that.

> Years later Joseph's brothers asked him to forgive them for what they had done. Joseph not only accepted the apology, but he also promised his brothers that he would take care of their children.

When you apologize for the things you have done wrong, you take responsibility for your actions. By doing so, you make it so that something good will come out of the mistakes you have made.

James 5:16 says:

> *So confess your sins to one another. Pray for one another so that you might be healed The prayer of a godly person is powerful Things happen because of it.*

When you choose to ask for forgiveness or to tell someone that you have sinned, your heart will be healed, and God can answer your prayers.

The Lesson

1 John 1:8-9 says:

> *Suppose we claim we are without sin. Then we are fooling ourselves. The truth is not in us. But God is faithful and fair. If we confess our sins, he will forgive our sins. He will forgive every wrong thing we have done. He will make us pure.*

What does this verse say will happen when we admit we have sinned?

- ○ Have the children share their answers.

- • God would forgive us our every wrong things we have done and make us pure. If I say, "I do not sin (lie, steal, hurt others, get angry etc.)," am I telling you the truth?
- ○ o Have the children share their thoughts.

- • No, because everyone sins.

When I tell God about my anger and apologize, does He forgive me?

- ○ Have the children share their thoughts.

- • Yes, God forgives me.

How about you? Do you have sins?

- ○ Have the children share their thoughts.

- • Give an appropriate example to the children of a time when you sinned.

When you tell God about your sins and choose to apologize, does He forgive you?

- ○ Have the children share their thoughts.

- • Yes, God will not only forgive you of your sins, but He also cleanses you from the things that made you do sin.

- • If you think you have made bad choices, the first thing you should do is apolo gize and ask God for forgiveness.

Activities

DRAW A PICTURE

Draw a picture of Joseph's brother's throwing him into a pit.

Draw a picture of Joseph forgiving his brothers and taking care of their families.

Share With the Children

Below are sentences for YOU to complete and share with the children. Pick one or two of them and share your own thoughts with the children. Ask the Holy Spirit and share appropriate examples or your testimonies.

- It was very difficult for me to apologize or ask for forgiveness because…

- The Holy Spirit helped me to apologize to…

- When I apologized I felt…

- When my friend asked me to forgive him/her, I felt…

Fun Time

Games

- **"Scene 1. Take 1"**

 someone hiding in a cave, playing cymbals, shooting flaming arrows, drinking from a fountain, turning water into wine, surfing on waves, Lazarus rising from the dead, someone watching a shooting star

- **Draw for the Master**

 a lady having a tea in her garden, a boy catching a hot dog, a family in a supermarket, people eating tacos, a banana tree, oranges and pineapples in a basket on a table with three legs, Zacchaeus climbing on a tree to see Jesus,

- **The Secret Object**

- **Paper Dash**

7.2 MAKING GOOD CHOICES
CHOOSING TO "FORGIVE"

Welcome
5'

Find out about the children. Share your answers first.

- Ask children what they did during the week,
- Find out what children had for a snack today.
- Ask them what kind of cookies they like.

Icebreaker Share your answers first.

- If you could give anything to your best friend, what would you give and why?

Books of the Week

Name The Books
5'

1ST & 2ND THESSALONIANS
1ST & 2ND TIMOTHT

Process

TEACHER

1) Introduce the Books
2) Say them like a _____
3) Repeat in groups
4) Skip repetition

STUDENTS

Say the names of the books in the Bible by yourself and get a sticker!

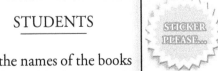

STICKER PLEASE...

Word: Lesson Objectives

Children think adults do not have to forgive people.
Share an appropriate story of an occasion when you forgave someone. Share how difficult it was and how God helped you in this process.

The Lesson

<u>Today we are going to make another good choice, which is to "forgive."</u>
Have you ever felt unhappy?
What are some of the things that make you unhappy?
 ○ Have the children share their answers.
Did you know that the Bible tells us not to make the Holy Spirit sad? Ephesians 4:30 says:

> *Do not make God's Holy Spirit mourn. The Holy Spirit is the proof that you belong to God And the Spirit is the proof that God will set you completely free.*

- The Holy Spirit is God's Spirit, and He is a person.

- The Holy Spirit has feelings just like we do.

- He feels sad when we do certain things.

Can you guess some of the things that might make the Holy Spirit sad?
 ○ Have the children share their thoughts.
Ephesians 4:31-32 says:

> *Get rid of all hard feeling anger and rage. Stop all fighting and lying. Don't have anything to do with any kind of hatred Be kind and tender to one another. Forgive one another, just as God forgave you because of what Christ has done.*

What are hard feelings?
 ○ Have the children share their thoughts.

- When you have hard feelings toward someone, you do not like what he or she has done or said to you, and you keep remembering what they did.

What are anger and rage?
 ○ Have the children share their thoughts.

- Anger is a feeling that you feel when you think someone did something wrong to you. Anger is an unfriendly attitude, and rage is a violent anger.

Have you ever felt angry?
 ○ Have the children share their experiences.

- When you get angry or throw a temper tantrum, you grieve the Holy Spirit.

Have you ever had a fight with someone?
- ○   Have the children share their experiences.

- •   When you fight with someone, you also grieve the Holy Spirit.

Ephesians also says we should stop lying.

What is lying?
- ○   Have the children share their answers.

- •   Lying is saying something that is not true on purpose to trick somebody. Listen to Ephesians 4:31-32 again.

> *Get rid of all hard feelings, anger and rage. Stop all fighting and lying. Don't have anything to do with any kind of hatred Be kind and tender to one an other. Forgive one another, just as God forgave you because of what Christ has done.*

How many angry thoughts, lies, or hateful thoughts do we need to get rid of? Do we need to get rid of only one of them?
- ○   Have the children share their thoughts.

- •   No, we need to get rid of "all of them."

- •   Instead of keeping anger, lies, or hatred in your heart, God wants you to tell Him about them and forgive the person who made you feel that way.

> People did mean and horrible things to Jesus. They spit on Him, called Him names, and put Him on the cross.

How would you feel if someone did those things to you?
- ○   Have the children share their thoughts.

Do you remember what Jesus said to the people who were mean to Him?

Luke 23:24 says:

> *Jesus said, "Father, forgive them. They don't know what they are doing."*

Ephesians 4:32 says:

> *"Forgive one another, just as God forgave you because of what Christ has done."*

When you choose to forgive, something wonderful happens in your heart. You will not grieve the Holy Spirit, and your heart will become more and more like Jesus's heart—kind and affectionate.

Would you like to get rid of all hard feelings, anger, and rage?
- Have the children share their answers.

Would you like to stop all fighting and lying?
- Have the children share their answers.

Would you like to put away every form of hatred?
- Have the children share their answers.

Do you have anyone you need to forgive?
- Have the children share their answers.

- If you are angry with someone, tell God you will forgive this person.

- Say, "God I forgive____(name)____ for _____."

- Ifyou have a difficult time forgiving, ask God to help you forgive this person.

God also wants us to ask Him for forgiveness when we sin. 1 John 1:8-9 says:

> *"God is faithful and fair. If we confess our sins, he will forgive our sins. He w!II forgive every wrong thing we have done. He will make us pure. 11*

If you would like to be forgiven, pray like this:
"God, I am sorry for feeling very angry at _____. Please forgive me."

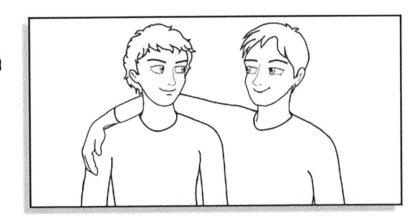

Activities

DRAW A PICTURE

Draw a face of a person who is angry and grieving the Holy Spirit.

Draw a face of someone who chose to forgive and the Holy Spirit giving the person a pure heart.

Share With the Children

Below are sentences for YOU to complete and share with the children. Pick one or two of them and share your own thoughts with the children. Ask the Holy Spirit and share appropriate examples or your testimonies.

- I asked God to forgive me for (getting angry, lying, holding on to hard feelings).

- When I admitted my sin, I felt God forgave me because...

- It was difficult for me to forgive (my friend) because...

- When I chose to forgive (my friend), I felt...

Games

Fun Time

- **"Draw it"**

a hammer, the ten commandments, a bride and a groom, a sponge, a broom, knees, a lock, a tree, a flag, a rainbow, an angel, a rat, an onion, a sink, a pair of shoes, a spotless sheep, a sweater

- **Who/What am I?**

Occupation: teacher, doctor, policeman, sales clerk, fireman, nurse, doctor, dentist, chef, plumber, bus driver, pilot, fisherman, carpenter, actor/actress, writer, movie director, astronaut, dancer, fashion designer

- **Card Games**

- **Where is the delivery?**

7.3 MAKING GOOD CHOICES
CHOOSING TO "OBEY YOUR PARENTS"

Welcome

Find out about the children. Share your answers first.

- Ask children what they did during the week,
- Find out where children's favorite places are and why.
- Ask how often they would like to be at their favorite places

Icebreaker Share your answers first.

- If you could go anywhere in the world, where would you go and why?

Name The Books

Books of the Week

_____IEW, MARK, LUKE, JOHN, ACTS, ROMANS, 1ST & 2ND CORINTHIANS, GALATIANS, EPHESIANS, PHILIPPIANS, COLOSSIANS, 1ST & 2ND THESSALONIANS, 1ST & 2ND TIMOTHY

Process

TEACHER	STUDENTS
1) Ask for a volunteer to recite alone or with friends. 2) Take a video 3) Encourage & reward!	Say the names of the books in the Bible by yourself and get a sticker!

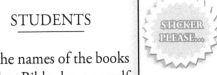

STICKER PLEASE...

Word: Lesson Objectives

Children think adults do not have to submit or obey. They think adults are not fair. Share with children an appropriate story of how you obeyed your parents as a child. Share how you submit to people in authority.

The Lesson

Today we will talk about obeying your parents.

Ephesians 6:1-3 says:

> *Chlfdren, obey your parents as believers in the Lord Obey them because it's the right thing to do. Scripture says, "Honor your father and mother." That is the first commandment that hasa promise. "Then things will go well with you. You wlfl live a long time on the earth."*

Colossians 3:20 says:

> *Children, obey your parents in everything. That pleases the Lord*

When someone is obedient to his or her parents, what does he or she do?

o   Have the children share their thoughts.

•   They pay attention to what their parents are saying and do what their parents are telling them to do.

According to these verses, why do we need to respect and pay attention to our parents?

o   Have the children share their thoughts.

•   When we respect our parents, pay attention to them, listen carefully to what they say, and do what they tell us to do, we please God-we make Him proud.

•   God is also concerned about our futures. He wants us to be healthy and live a long life. That is why He wants us to listen to our parents and do what they tell you to do.

When people obey their parents, do they act like they did not hear them?

o   Have the children share their thoughts.

•   People who obey their parents listen carefully and act exactly as their parents wish.

When your parents tell you to pick up trash on the floor, what does God want you to do?

o   Have the children share their thoughts.

•   God would want us to pick up trash because he wants us to obey our parents.

•   To obey or not to obey your parents is a choice you make.

•   We want to keep making "good choices."

Pop Quiz! Which one is the right choice?

When parents tell you to pick up your socks on the floor, you…

a) Keep watching your TV show and tell them you will do it later.

b) Stop watching your TV show and pick up your socks right away.

c) Pretend you did not hear your parents.

Proverbs 6:20 says:

My son, keep your father's commands.
Don't turn away from your mother's teaching.

What are some of the commands your father gives you?

o   Have the children share their answers.

o   Share an appropriate example of something your father told you to do.

What are some teachings your mother gives you?

o   Have the children share their thoughts.

o   Children need to know you had to obey your father's command when you were a child.

o   Share an appropriate example of something your mother taught you.

Proverbs 6:21 says:

Always tie them (father's commands) on your heart. Put them around your neck.

What are you supposed to do with what your parents tell you to do?

•   Tie their words to your heart and put them around your neck forever.

What does tying what your parents teach you around your heart mean?

o   Have the children share their thoughts.

•   It means to always be mindful of their teachings.

What does putting them around your neck mean?

o   Have the children share their thoughts.

•   It means to always remember what your parents say.

•   When your parents tell you to say "please" when you are asking for something, you must always remember to say "please."

Proverbs 6:22 says:

When you walk, they will gwde you. When you sleep, they will watch over you. When you wake up, they will speak to you.

When would the things your parents tell you to do help you?

o   Have the children share their thoughts.

•   They will keep you safe when you sleep and speak to you when you are awake.

Proverbs 6:23 says:

> *Your father's command is like a lamp. Your mother's teaching is ltke a light. And whatever instructs and corrects you leads to life.*

What is your father's command like?

- It is like a lamp or like a flashlight-a bright beam of light.

Have you ever used a flashlight in the dark?

◦ Have the children share their experiences and talk about what the flashlights did for them.

- God is saying that what your father commands you to do is like a flashlight for you.

- What your father tells you to do will help guide you and keep you safe.

What is your mother's teaching like?

- It is like a light.

- What your mother tells you will protect you and help you understand things better.

God is always watching. He will reward you for obeying your parents even when they are not watching.

◦ Share with children that there will be temptations to disobey when their parents (or other people) are not watching.

DRAW A PICTURE

Draw a picture of yourself, paying attention to what your parents tell you to do.

Ask God

Ask God how He feels about you when you pay attention to your parents and do what they ask you to do.

Share With the Children

Below are sentences for YOU to complete and share with the children. Pick one or two of them and share your own thoughts with the children. Ask the Holy Spirit and share appropriate examples or your testimonies.

- One of the things my Father taught me is…
- One of the things my Mother taught me is…
- When I disobeyed my parents I felt…
- When I obeyed my parents I felt…
- Share how you learned to obey your parents.

Games

Fun Time

- **Telephone**

  - the proof of the pudding is in the eating.
  - If you don't stand for something you will fall for something. You have to do your own growing no matter how tall your grandfather was.
  - It is God who changes the world, not me.
  - Intelligent children listen to their parents; foolish children do their own thing

- **Paper Planes**

- **I Found My Dentures!**

- **The Guardian**

8.1 MAKING MORE GOOD CHOICES
CHOOSING TO "SERVE"

Welcome 5'

Find out about the children. Share your answers first.

- Ask children what they did during the week,
- Find out what children's favorite toys are and how the children plays with them.
- Find out how the children got the toy.

Icebreaker   Share your answers first.

- If you owned a toy company, what kind of toy/toys would you make and sell?

Name The Books 5'

TITUS

PHILEMON

HEBREWS

JAMES

Process

TEACHER	STUDENTS
1) Introduce the Books 2) Repeat in groups 3) Skip repetition 4) Keep the beat	Say the names of the books in the Bible by yourself and get a sticker!

Children do not perceive serving as a positive thing. They also think adults do not have to serve. Share with children how serving can be difficult for you also, but how it can bring joy to your heart.

The Lesson

Today we are going to talk about serving.
What is serving? When you serve someone, what do you do?
- ○ Have the children share their answers.

- • To serve means to offer a meal or refreshments, to be useful, give something that a person needs or to help.

Philippians 2:4 says:

> None of you should look out just for your own good You should also look out for the good of others.

What do you think this verse is trying to say?
- ○ Have the children share their thoughts.

- • Paul is teaching that none of us should be thinking only about ourselves.

- • The Bible says we should look out for the good of others.

What do people do when they are looking out for the good of others?
- ○ Have the children share their thoughts.
- ○ Share your thoughts with the children.

- • • People would share things, encourage, be helpful, treat people nicely, or send gifts.

Do you care for other people? Who do you care about?
- ○ Have the children share their answers.

Pop quiz!
Raise your hand if you think Jimmy is looking out for the good of others in each of these situations.

> 1. Jimmy saw his brother's toy on the floor, so he picked it up and put it away for his brother.
> (Yes, Jimmy was thoughtful enough to look out for the good of his brother.)
> 2. Jimmy saw his brother's toy on the floor but did not care to put it away for his brother, because it was not Jimmy's toy.
> (No, Jimmy did not think of helping out his brother.)

3. Jimmy had a candy and threw his candy wrapper on the floor.
(No, Jimmy is not trying to keep the floor clean because he does not care about how other people may feel.)
4. Jimmy waited patiently for the lady with a walker to get by at a grocery store. (Yes, Jimmy was thoughtful and kind to the lady with walker. He waited patiently so she would not have to rush.)
5. Jimmy saw an older lady with a walker. She was very slow, so he ran by her as fast as he could so that he would not have to wait for her to get by.
(No, Jimmy is thinking only about himself and not about the lady.)
6. Jimmy saw that there was not enough mac-and-cheese for everyone, so he served himself a plate full of mac-and-cheese before anyone else and enjoyed it all by himself.
(No, Jimmy is thinking only about himself and not about people who is lining up behind him who might like to have some mac-and cheese.)
7. Jimmy saw that there was not enough mac-and-cheese for everyone, so he served a small portion for himself so that everyone else could enjoy mac-and cheese as well.
(Yes, Jimmy is very considerate. He would like others to have Mac-and-cheese so he decided to save some for them to enjoy.)
8. Jimmy thanked his mother for dinner, took his plate to the sink and washed them.
(Yes, Jimmy thought of his mother who spent time cooking for him and did his dishes so his mother would not have to clean them.)
9. Jimmy simply left the table when he was done eating and played his video game. (No, Jimmy was not thankful or thoughtful of others.)

o   Additional discussion ideas:
What would you suggest that Jimmy do?
Why would you suggest that he do that?

Philippian 2:6b-7 says:

> *Jesus was equal with God But Jesus didn't take advantage of that fact Instead, he made himself nothing. He did this by taking on the nature of a servant*

Mark 10:45 says:

Even the Son of Man dtd not come to be served Instead, he came to serve others. He came to give his life as the price for setting many people free.

Galatians 5:13 says:

> *My brothersand sisters, you were chosen to be free. But don't use your freedom asan excuse to live under the power of sin. Instead, serve one another in love.*

Mathew 20:26 says:

> *Anyone who wants to be important among you must be your servant*

Let's think of ways you can serve the people around you.
- ○ Help the children think of services they can apply right away.
- • Examples: Offering to help with the dishes, holding doors for people, letting friends go first, sweeping the neighbor's walkway, sharpening pencils for the teacher.

How can you serve your family (dad, mom, grandparents, brothers, sisters)?
- ○ Have the children share their ideas.
- ○ Share with the children how you serve your family.

How can you serve your friends?
- ○ Have the children share their ideas.
- ○ Share with the children how you serve your friends.

How can you serve your neighbors?
- ○ Have the children share their ideas.
- ○ Share with the children how you serve your neighbors.

How can you serve your teachers?
- ○ Have the children share their ideas.
- ○ Share with the children how you serve your boss or person in authority.

Ephesians 6:7-8 says:

> *Serve your masters with all your heart. Work as serving the Lord and not as serving people. You know that the Lord will give each person a reward He will give to them in keeping with the good they do. It doesn't matter whether they are a slave or not*

When we serve someone, we should serve them as if we were serving Jesus. Do you ever feel like not serving?

- o Have the children share their experiences.
- o Share your experience.

What can we do when we do not feel like serving and we begin to complain?

- o Have the children share their thoughts.
- o Share what you do when you do not feel like serving.

- • When we complain about serving or do not want to serve for others, we are be ing very selfish.

- • When we become selfish, we should repent and ask God to change our hearts.

DRAW A PICTURE

Draw a picture of yourself, serving your family. What can you do for them?

Ask God

Ask God how you can serve your family. Share with God what you would like to do for your family.

Share With the Children

Below are sentences for YOU to complete and share with the children. Pick one or two of them and share your own thoughts with the children. Ask the Holy Spirit and share appropriate examples or your testimonies.

- When I was a child, my chores were…
- I serve (my family, friends, community, and people at work) by…
- When I do not feel like serving I… (share what you do).
- Share stories of people who have a heart of servant that you admire.

Games

- **"Scene 1. Take 1"**

Jesus calms the storm, ravens (birds) bringing bread,
a person eating a whole apple, a monkey riding a bike,
a person drinking a very hot tea,
someone picking up a coin from the ground

- **Draw for the Master**

a baked potato on a plate, a doctor with a lollipop,
a bird flying over a desert, a dozen eggs in a hat on a tree, a policeman drinking coffee, a lion wearing sunglasses lounging on a beach,
a giraffe on a swing

- **The Secret Object**

- **Masking Tape Activities**

Notes

8.2 MAKING MORE GOOD CHOICES
CHOOSING TO "GIVE"

Welcome
5′

Find out about the children. Share your answers first.

- Ask children what they did during the week,
- Find out what kind of lessons children are taking.
- Find out if they enjoy the activity or not and why the like or dislike the activity.

Icebreaker   Share your answers first.

- If you could be really good at one thing you cannot do yet, what would that be and why?

Books of the Week

Name The Books

5′

THEW, MARK, LUKE, JOHN,
ACTS, ROMANS, 1ST & 2ND CORINTHIANS,
GALATIANS, EPHESIANS PHILIPPIANS,
COLOSSIANS, 1ST & 2ND THESSALONIANS,
1ST & 2ND TIMOTHY, TITUS,
PHILEMON, HEBREWS, JAMES

Process

TEACHER	STUDENTS
1) Ask for a volunteer to recite alone or with friends. 2) Take a video 3) Encourage & reward!	Say the names of the books in the Bible by yourself and get a sticker!

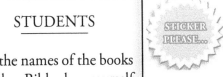

STICKER PLEASE...

Word: Lesson Objectives

Foster a generous heart in children. Share an appropriate example of a time when you had difficulty giving to others. Share how you bless others by giving or how you have been blessed by someone who gave generously to you.

The Lesson

<u>**Today we are going to talk about giving.**</u>
Have you ever given something to someone?
- o   Have the children share their experiences.

How did giving something make you feel?
- o   Have the children share how they felt.

- •   A heart that does not want to give or share is a selfish heart.

Were there times you did not feel like giving or sharing?
- o   Share an appropriate example of a time when you did not feel like giving or sharing.
- o   Have the children share their experiences.

In 2 Corinthians 9:6 Paul compares giving with planting seeds. It says,

> *Here is something to remember. The one who plants onlya little will gather onlyalittle. And the one who plants a lot will gather a lot.*

Who gathers only a little?
- o   Have the children share their answers.

- •   A person who plants or gives only a little will gather only a little.

Who gathers a lot?
- o   Have the children share their answers.

- •   A person who plants or gives a lot will gather a lot.
- o   Discuss how one sunflower seed can produce eight hundred to two thousand seeds.

Why does God multiply what we give to other people?
- o   Have the children share their thoughts.

- •   God multiplies when we give so that we can give more!

We have been learning about making good choices. Giving is also a choice you make. 2 Corinthians 9:7 says:

> *Vou should each give what you have decided in your heart to give. You shouldn't give if you don't want to. You shouldn't give because you are forced to.*

Have you ever felt upset when your mother told you to give some of your candies to your siblings or your friends?

- ○ Share an appropriate experience of a time when you did not want to share.
- ○ Have the children share their experiences.

- • God is telling us that we all have to make a choice to give or not to give.

- • When we give, He wants us to be happy about it.

2 Corinthians 9:7c says:

> *"God loves a cheerful giver."*

What does a cheerful giver look like?

- ○ Have the children share their thoughts.

- • A cheerful giver is someone who is so happy to give.

By giving, you can be a part of building God's Kingdom and receive blessings from God! We can make other people happy!

Have you ever seen a cheerful giver?

- ○ Share about a cheerful giver you have met.

- • Have the children share their experiences.

Would you like to be a cheerful giver?

- ○ Have the children share their thoughts.

Let's ask God to give us a heart to give and be a cheerful giver.

- ○ Pray with the children.

2 Corinthians 9:8 says:

> *And God is able to shower all kinds of blessings on you. So in all things and at all times you will have everything you need Vou will do more and more good works.*

When we choose to give, what can God do for us?

- ○ Have the children share their thoughts.

- • He showers all kinds of blessings on us.

Will we be sad because we do not have the things we need?

○   Have the children share their thoughts.

•   No, we will not be sad because we will have everything we need. 2 Corinthians 9:12 says:

> *Your gifts meet the needs of the Lord's people. And that's not all. Your gifts also cause many people to thank God*

What would the things or money you give do?

○   Have the children share their thoughts.

•   The gifts we give will meet the need of others.

Acts 20:35 says:

> *In everything I did, I showed you that we must work hard and help the weak. We must remember the words of the Lord Jesus. He said, "It is more blessed to give than to receive."*

Acts 20:35 says:

> *It is more blessed to give than to receive.*

In the Bible there is another kind of giving called the "tithe."

•   Tithing is giving back what belongs to God.

•   God says we rob God when we do not give one tenth of what we have earned.

•   Explain one tenth: When you earn ten dollars for washing a car, you give one dollar back to God.

When we do not tithe (give one tenth back to God), we are robbing God, and He cannot bless us with more. When we do not follow God's way, we will not be blessed or protected. Life without God's protection is under a curse. God wants to protect us. We need to choose to give back to God so He can protect us and bless us.

What do you think God promises to do when we give our tithe back to God?

○   Have the children share their thoughts.

When we give one tenth back to God,

- *There will be plenty of food,*

- *He will throw open the windows of heaven,*

- *He w!II pour out so many blessings that you will not have enough room for them, keep bugs from eating up your food,*

- *All of the nations will callyou blessed and our country w!II be delightful.*

(Malachi 3:10-12)

What would you like to give others?
- ○ Have the children share their thoughts.

- Examples of ways to give: draw a picture for someone, share a snack, give a toy, help out, give a glass of water, give up your turn for someone else, or give a flower.

DRAW A PICTURE

Draw a picture of yourself, giving a gift to someone you care.

Ask God

Share with the Lord what you would like to give to your parents. Ask God what you can give to your family or friends.

You received one hundred dollars from your grandmother for your birthday. How much should you tithe?

$100

$50   **$20**   **$10**

$5   **$1**   **$1**

$1   **$1**   **$1**

Draw a picture of someone who is happy to give.

5'

Below are sentences for YOU to complete and share with the children. Pick one or two of them and share your own thoughts with the children. Ask the Holy Spirit and share appropriate examples or your testimonies.

- I give to people who are in need because…

- I want to become a person who loves to give because…

- When I gave God provided. (Share your testimony)

- I learned the words in Malachi are true. (Share your conviction)

Fun Time

Games

10+

- **"Draw it"**

 a raft, leaves, ground, a castle, horseback, a boat, an ice cube, a rope, paint, a family, a grasshopper, a glass of water, left hand a farmer, a banana, a coin, a pig, cherries

- **Who/What am I?**

 Animals: cheetah, anteater, deer, peacock, dolphin, elephant, horse, fox, hippopotamus, koala, flamingo, snake, turtle, duck, porcupine, rhinoceros, rabbit, sloth, whale, frog

- **Card Games**

- **Super Toes**

8.2 MAKING MORE GOOD CHOICES
CHOOSING TO "HONOR YOUR PARENTS"

Welcome — 5'

Find out about the children. Share your answers first.

- Ask children what they did during the week.
- Find out what children's favorite songs are.
- Find out where they learned the song and who they sing the song with.

Icebreaker   Share your answers first.

- If you had to give all of your toys away but allowed to keep one favorite toy, which one would you keep and why?

Name The Books — 5'

Books of the Week

Review the Books in the Old Testament

GENESIS, EXODUS, LEVITICUS NUMBERS
DEUTERONOMY, JOSHUA, JUDGES, RUTH 1ST & 2ND
SAMUEL, 1ST & 2ND KINGS, 1ST & 2ND CHRONICLES,
EZRA, NEHEMIAH, ESTHER, JOB, PSALMS, PROVERBS,
ECCLESIASTES, SONG OF SOLOMON, ISAIAH, JEREMIAH,
LAMENTATIONS, EZEKIEL, DANIEL, HOSEA, JOEL,
AMOS, OBADIAH, JONAH, MICAH, NAHUM, HABAKKUK,
ZEPHANIAH, HAGGAI, ZECHARIAH, MALACHI

Process

TEACHER	STUDENTS
1) Ask for a volunteer to recite alone or with friends. 2) Take a video 3) Encourage & reward!	Say the names of the books in the Bible by yourself and get a sticker!

STICKER PLEASE...

This lesson teaches children about honoring their parents. Children think adults do not have to honor anyone. Share with children how you honor your parents or people in authority.

The Lesson

Today we will talk about choosing to honor your parents.

Have you ever heard of the word "honor"?

Have you ever honored someone?
- ○ Have the children share their answers.

When you honor someone, how do you feel about this person?
- ○ Have the children share their thoughts.

- • When you honor someone you show the person great respect and give them special attention.

Exodus 20:12 says:

> *Honor your father and mother. Then you willlive a long time in the land the LORD your God is giving you.*

Who does God want us to honor?
- ○ Have the children share their answers.

- • God wants us to honor our parents.

What does the Scripture say about children who honor their parents?
- ○ Have the children share their answers.

- • They will live a long time in the land God gives them.

- • When you honor your parents, you will live long, which probably means you will stay healthy and safe for a long time.

What do you think God told the Israelites to do to children who do not honor their parents?
- ○ Have the children share their thoughts.

Exodus 21:15-17 says:

> *Anyone who attacks their father or mother must be put to death. "Anyone who kidnaps and sells another person must be put to death. If they sttll have the person with them when they are caught, they must be put to death." Anyone who asks for something bad to happen to their father or mother must be put to death*

What does the Scripture say about children who attack their parents or talks disrespectfully to their parents?
- ○ Have the children share their answers.
- • The Scripture says that they will be put to death.
- • This might sound scary, but this is how much God wants you to honor your parents.
- • He wants to make sure you honor your parents, because He loves you, and He wants you to be safe and to live for a long time.

There are many ways we can honor your parents.
Let's think of ways you can honor your parents.

How can we honor our parents?
- ○ Have the children share their ideas.
- • Share with children how you honor your parents.

We can honor our parents by
- • listening to them very carefully
- • greeting them everyday
- • saying thank you
- • introducing them to your friends
- • offering them to be served first
- • opening doors for them

If you want something at the store, do you ask for it, demand it, or whine until you get it?
- ○ Have the children share their thoughts.
- • Whining or being demanding in order to get someone to do something for you is called manipulation.
- • Whining or being demanding is not honoring that person.
- • At times it's okay to ask nicely for something you'd like-but notall the time.

When your parents are talking, what can you do to honor them? (Pick one that applies.)
1. Talk back.
2. Talk over your parents.
3. Ignore them.
4. Look into their eyes and listen until they are done talking.

o   Share with children an appropriate example of a time you did not honor your parents and how you learned to honor your parents.

•   It might take a lot of practice but you really need to listen without talking back to your parents.

•   When you learn to listen to your parents, you will be able to listen to other peo ple too. That is being respectful.

•   You can honor your parents by telling them you love them.

Do you tell your parents that you love them?
o   Have the children share their answers.

•   Make sure they know that you do love them.

Tell your parents you love them every night before bed, every morning before going to school, before you hang up the phone, and before they leave the house to go to work or to go shopping.

Have you ever given gifts to your parents?
o   Have the children share their experiences.

•   You can honor your parents by giving them presents.

Giving gifts is a sign that you honor them for what they are doing for you (laundry, cooking, buying things you need, and driving you around). Giving gifts is a sign that you remember that they are there and you love them.

Color the Picture

Activities

DRAW A PICTURE

Draw a picture of yourself, honoring your parents.

Ask God

Ask the Holy Spirit how you can honor God. Ask God how you can honor your parents.

Share With the Children

Below are sentences for YOU to complete and share with the children. Pick one or two of them and share your own thoughts with the children. Ask the Holy Spirit and share appropriate examples or your testimonies.

- I honor my parents by… (Share how you honor your parents.)
- I think honoring your parents is very important because…
- I choose to honor people because…
- When I do not feel like honoring someone I… (Share what you do.)

Fun Time

Games

- **"Draw it"**

  - As clear as a bell, as clear as crystal, as clear as day, as clear as mud
  - Birds of a feather flock together.
  - My friend brought everything from soup to nuts for the camping trip.
  - It doesn't matter what you look like on outside…It's what is on the in side that counts.
  - The Fear of God is a spring of living water.

- **Paper Planes**

- **I Found My Dentures!**

- **Mission Balance**

9.1 MAKING MORE GOOD CHOICES
CHOOSING TO "HONOR YOUR PARENTS"

Welcome

5'

Find out about the children. Share your answers first.

- Ask children what they did during the week.
- Find out one thing children learned at school today.
- Find out who the most wisest person in his or her school is.

Icebreaker   Share your answers first.

- If you could tell your mom never to serve two vegetables again, which two would you choose?

Name The Books

5'

1ST & 2ND PETER
1ST, 2ND & 3RD JOHN
JUDE
REVELATION

Process

TEACHER	STUDENTS
1) Introduce the Books 2) Repeat in groups 3) Skip repetition 4) Keep the beat	Say the names of the books in the Bible by yourself and get a sticker!

Word: Lesson Objectives

Children learn to praise God by watching you praise God. Share with children why you worship God. Help children develop their language to praise and worship God.

 The Lesson

<u>Today we are going to talk about praising God.</u>
How do you know if a person is praising God?
- ○ Have the children share their thoughts.

- • Praise means to speak well of someone or something or to honor with words or song.

  King David knew he was loved by God, and he loved God, so he praised God all his life. God said David was a man after His own heart.

- ○ Have the children listen to the Psalm carefully and answer these questions.
In Psalm 27:4, David said,
> *I'm asking the LORD for only one thing. Here is what I want*
> *I want to live in the house of the LORD all the days of my life.*
> *I want to look at the beauty of the LORD.*
> *I want to worship him in his temple.*

What does David want to do?
- ○ Have the children share their thoughts.

- • He wants to live in the house of the LORD all the days of his life.

What does David want to see?
- ○ Have the children share their thoughts.

- • He wants to look at the beauty of the LORD.

What does he want to do in God's temple?
- ○ Have the children share their thoughts.

- • He wants to worship Him.

When someone worships God, what do you think this person says to God?
- ○ Have the children share their thoughts.

- • When you worship God, you are showing Him how much you love Him.

- • There are different ways you can express how you feel about Him.

The Lesson

What are some of the ways of worship you know?
- ○ Have the children share their thoughts.

- • Examples: singing, dancing, painting, drawing, writing, staying still in His pres ence.

Close your eyes and listen to Psalm 104:1.

> *I will praise the LORD.*
> *LORD my God, you are vety great*
> *You are dressed in gloty and majesty.*

What did you see?
- ○ Have the children share what they saw.

What did David see?

- • David saw God dressed in glory and majesty.

- • David saw God's greatness.

Do you think God is great? Why do you think so?
- ○ Have the children share their thoughts.
- ○ Share why you think God is great and why you worship Him.

Close your eyes again and listen to verses 2-4.

> *the LORD wraps himself in light as if it were a robe.*
> *He spreads out the heavens like a tent.*
> *He builds his palace high in the heavens.*
> *He makes the clouds serve as his chariot.*
> *He rides on the wings of the wind*
> *He makes the winds serve as his messengers.*
> *He makes flashes of lightning serve him.*

How did David see God?

- • God was wrapped in light. It looked like He was wearing a robe made of light.

What is God clothed in?

- • He is clothed in light.

What did God spread?

- • He spread the heavens.

Where does God build His palace?

- • He builds his palace high in the heavens.

What does God ride?

- • He rides on the clouds.

What can God do to the winds and flashes of lightening?

- • He commands the winds, directs them as he pleases, and makes them serve Him for His own purposes.

Close your eyes and listen to verses 5-9.

> *He placed the earth on its foundations. It can neverbe moved*
> *You, LORD, covered it with the oceans like a blanket*
> *The waters covered the mountains.*
> *But you commanded the waters, and they ran away.*
> *At the sound of your thunder they rushed off*
> *They flowed down the mountains.*
> *They went into the valleys.*
> *They went to the place you appointed for them.*
> *You drewa line they can't cross.*
> *They will never cover the earth again.*

What story in the Bible is David thinking about?

- ◦ Have the children share their thoughts.

- • He is thinking about the flood.

What is David praising God for?

- ◦ Have the children share their thoughts.

- • David is praising God because God has the authority to keep water from going wherever it wants to.

Close your eyes again and listen to verses 10-12.

> *The LORD makes springs pour water into the valleys.*
> *It flows between the mountains.*
> *The springs give water to all the wild animals.*
> *The wild donkeys satisfy their thirst*
> *The birds in the sky build nestsby the waters.*
> *They sing among the branches.*

What is David praising God for?

- ◦ Have the children share their thoughts.

- • David is praising God for making water that sustains life on earth, including us.

- • Most animals that live on land need fresh water to live.

- • David wrote about wild donkeys and birds as examples.

What kinds of animals need water? Who gives them water to drink?

- • God gives water to every living thing on earth. Let's praise God for giving water to all of the wild animals.

- • Example: "God, You give water to every animal! That is amazing!"

Close your eyes again and listen to verses 13-14.

> *The LORD waters the mountains from his palace high in the clouds.*
> *The earth is hl/ed with the things he has made.*
> *He makes grass grow for the cattle and plants for people to take care of*
> *That's how they get food from the earth.*

Imagine God's palace that can keep water to pour on earth.

What does it look like?

- ° o Have the children share their thoughts.

Worship is a choice we make. When we go to church and worship, we worship with other people who know the Creator of heaven and earth. We worship Him for many different reasons, but it is a choice we make. When we choose to worship God, it gives great joy to God.

Activities

DRAW A PICTURE

Close your eyes, listen to Psalm 104 verses 5–4 and draw a picture of the scene.

Below are sentences for YOU to complete and share with the children. Pick one or two of them and share your own thoughts with the children. Ask the Holy Spirit and share appropriate examples or your testimonies.

- I praise God because…

- When I choose to praise God I feel…

- Share testimonies of how your praise changed a situation.

- Share what giving praises to God means to you.

Games

10+

- **"Scene 1. Take 1"**

Jesus healing the sick, a hungry caterpillar, someone climbing a mountain, a giraffe drinking water, a very thirsty person, a rainbow, spreading hard butter on bread, someone riding a unicycle

- **Draw for the Master**

a bunny eating popcorn, a person in pajamas, a turtle on a table, a banana with round eyes wearing a sombrero, a fancy chair, an ice cream in a bowl falling from the sky,

- **The Secret Object**

- **Paper Dash**

Notes

9.2 PRAISE AND WORSHIP
GIVE MORE PRAISE TO GOD

Welcome 5'

Find out about the children. Share your answers first.

- Ask children what they did during the week.
- Find out who the children think is the funniest person they know.
- Ask why they think the person is funny.

Icebreaker   Share your answers first.

- What was the funniest thing that has happened to you?

Name The Books 5'

Encourage the children to recite the entire books in the New Testament.

MATTHEW, MARK, LUKE, JOHN,
ACTS, ROMANS, 1ST & 2ND CORINTHIANS,
GALATIANS, EPHESIANS, PHILIPPIANS,
COLOSSIANS, 1ST & 2ND THESSALONIANS,
1ST & 2ND TIMOTHY, TITUS, PHILEMON,
HEBREWS, JAMES, 1ST & 2ND PETER,
1ST, 2ND, & 3RD JOHN, JUDE, REVELATION

Process

TEACHER

1) Introduce the Books
2) Say them like a _____
3) Repeat in groups
4) Skip repetition

STUDENTS

Say the names of the books in the Bible by yourself and get a sticker!

STICKER PLEASE...

Word: Lesson Objectives

Children learn to praise God by watching you praise God. Share with children why you worship God. Help children develop their language to praise and worship God.

The Lesson

We are going to continue to praise God this week!
Last week we learned that David loved God and praised God all his life.
What do you remember about David and how he praised God?
  ○ Have the children share how David praised God.

  • David knew he was loved by God, and David loved Him back.

  • He wanted everything on earth to praise God.

Let's read Psalm 150.

> *Praise The LORD. Praise God in his holy temple.*
> *Praise him in his mighty heavens.*
> *Praise him for his powerful acts.*
> *Praise him because he is greater than anything else.*
> *Praise him by blowing trumpets.*
> *Praise him with harps and lyres.*
> *Praise him with tambourines and dancing.*
> *raise him with stringed instruments and flutes.*
> *Praise him with clashing cymbals.*
> *Let everything that has breath praise The LORD. Praise The LORD.*

What did David use to praise God?
  ○ David praised God with his instruments.
How would like to praise God?
  ○ Share how you would like to praise God.
  ○ Ask the children how they would like to praise God.

Let's read Psalm 104:24:

> *LORD, you have made so many things!*
> *How wise you were when you made all of them!*
> *The earth is full of your creatures.*

What is David praising God for?
  ○ Have the children share their thoughts.

  • David praised God for the creatures He has made.

The Lesson

Can you think of creatures God has made?

- Have the children take turns praising God for one creature.
  Example: "God, I praise you for making…

  - "cheetahs that can run so fast!"

  - "eagles that can fly so high!"

  - "dogs that are friendly!"

  - "horses, so people can ride on them!"

Let's read the next part. Psalm 104:25.

> *Look at the ocean, so big and wide!*
> *It is filled with more creatures than people can count*
> *It is filled with living things, from the largest to the smallest.*

Can you think of creatures in the ocean that God has made?

- Have the children take turns praising God for one oceanic creature.

Let's read Psalm 147:4:

> *He deodes how many stars there should be.*
> *He gives each one of them a name.*

How many stars are there in the universe?

- Have the children share their guesses.

- God gives a name to every star!

- Ask one or two children to praise God, for making the stars.

Let's continue to read Psalm 147:

> *Great is our Lord His power is mighty*
> *There is no limit to his understanding.*

Is there anything that is more powerful than God?

- Have the children share their thoughts.

- No, God is omnipotent.

- There is absolutely nothing His power cannot accomplish.

Does God know and understand everything?

- Have the children share their thoughts.

- Yes, God is omniscient.

- God has infinite understanding of everything.

Does He know what happened in the past, what is happening now, and what is go ing to happen in the future?

- Have the children share their answers.

- Yes, God is omnipresent.

God knows everything that happened in the past, everything that is happening now, and everything that is going to take place in the future.

- ○ Ask one or two children to praise God, who knows everything.
- ○ Revisit Unit 2, Lessons 1, 2, and 3, and see what the children wrote about God's omnipotence, omniscience, and omnipresence.

DRAW A PICTURE

Draw a picture of yourself, praising God with instruments.

Draw a picture of angels worshipping God and Jesus.

Below are sentences for YOU to complete and share with the children. Pick one or two of them and share your own thoughts with the children. Ask the Holy Spirit and share appropriate examples or your testimonies.

- I praise God even when I am having a bad day because...

- I learned to praise God... (Explain when, how and from who.)

- Share how you praise God.

- Share what you have learned from David.

Fun Time

Games

10+

- **"Draw it"**

   the universe, a web site, an ink bottle, a full moon, sore throat, milk and honey, an ark, a painting, an apple tree, a cumulous cloud, a seatbelt, a dress, a bed, a nail, breakfast, fried chicken

- **Who/What am I?**

   Fruit: oranges, grapes, raspberry, strawberry, lemon, cherry, peach, banana, melon, watermelon, kiwi, pineapple, apple, mango, pear, blueberries, grapefruit, cantaloupe, limes, apricot

- **Card Games**

- **Where is the delivery?**

9.3 PRAISE AND WORSHIP
THE THRONE OF GOD

Welcome
5'

Find out about the children. Share your answers first.

- Ask children what they did during the week.
- Find out where children spend time playing at school.
- Find out what playground equipment they like to play with.

Icebreaker Share your answers first.

- Who is the most courageous person you have ever met or have heard of?
- What did this person do?

Name The Books

5'

Books of the Week

GENESIS, EXODUS, LEVITICUS NUMBERS,
DEUTERONOMY, JOSHUA, JUDGES, RUTH
1ST & 2ND SAMUEL, 1ST & 2ND KINGS,
1ST & 2ND CHRONICLES, EZRA, NEHEMIAH,
ESTHER, JOB, PSALMS, PROVERBS, ECCLESIASTES,
SONG OF SOLOMON, ISAIAH, JEREMIAH,
LAMENTATIONS, EZEKIEL, DANIEL, HOSEA,
JOEL, AMOS, OBADIAH, JONAH, MICAH
NAHUM, HABAKKUK, ZEPHANIAH, HAGGAI,
ZECHARIAH, MALACHI

Review the Books in the Old Testament..

Next week we will have New Testament Extreme Challenge!

Process

TEACHER

1) Review the Books
2) Ask for a volunteer to recite alone or with friends.
3) Encourage & reward!

STUDENTS

Say the names of the books in the Bible by yourself and get a sticker!

STICKER PLEASE...

In this lesson the children will be introduced to the throne of God. Help them describe what the throne of God looks like. Share your thoughts about the throne of God.

Today we are going to see what God's throne looks like.
What is a throne?

o   Have the children share their thoughts.

•   Here on earth, a throne is a decorated seat where a king or queen sits for spe cial ceremonies. Ephesians 1:20b-21 says:

> *God seated Him (Jesus) at his right hand in his heavenly kingdom. There Christ sits far above all who rule and have authority. He also sits far above all powers and kings. He is above eve'Y name that is appealed to in this world and in the world to come.*

Have you ever thought of what a throne of God might look like?

o   Have the children share their answers.

Let's read Revelation 4:1-2.

> *After this I looked, and there in front of me was a door standing open in heaven. I heard the voice I had heard before. It sounded like a trumpet The voice said, "Come up here. I will show you what must happen after this.11 At once the Holy Spirit gave me a vision. There in front of me was a throne in heaven with someone sitting on it The one who sat there shone ltke jasper and ruby. Around the throne was a rainbow shining ltke an emerald*

What did John see?

•   He saw someone (God) sitting on the throne.

What did He look like?

•   The person sitting on the throne (God) shone like jewels.

What did John see around the throne?

•   He saw a rainbow that looked like an emerald.

What do rainbows remind you of?

o   Have the children share their thoughts.

•   Rainbows remind us of God's covenant to Noah that He would never destroy the earth with water (Gen. 9:13-16).

John says he saw the rainbow around the throne.

Do you think that this is the same kind of rainbow we see?
- o Have the children share their thoughts.
- • Can it be a rainbow that is all around the throne, not only on top of the throne? How does the idea of the throne of God surrounded by emerald rainbow make you feel?
- o Have the children share how they feel.
- o Share how it makes you feel.

In Hebrews 4:16, Pal says,

> *So let us boldly approach God's throne of grace. Then we will receive mercy We will find grace to help us when we need it.*

When we approach God's throne of grace, we will receive mercy.

When someone has mercy, what do you think that person is like?
- o Have the children share their thoughts.
- • When someone has mercy, he feels the other person's pain and act in kindness.
- • Mercy is kindness shown to a person who could be treated unforgivingly.
- • When we fear God and call on Him, we receive God's kindness.

How long will the throne of God be in heaven?
- o Have the children share their thoughts.
- • The throne of God is in heaven and will be in heaven forever and ever.

Daniel 7:14 says:

> *And he was given authority, glory and a kingdom. People of all nations, no matter what language they spoke, worshiped him. His authority will last forever. It will not pass away His kingdom will never be destroyed*

Psalm 45:6 says:

> *Your throne is the very throne of God*
> *Your kingdom will last for ever and ever*
> *You will rule by treating everyone fairly Forever and ever.*

One day we will stand in front of His throne.

Matthew 25:31-32 says:

> *"The Son of Man will come in all his glory All the angels will come with him.*
> *Then he will sit in glory on his throne. All the nations will be gathered in front of him.*

Activities

DRAW A PICTURE

Close your eyes and listen to Revelation chapter 4. Draw a picture of what you saw.

Below are sentences for YOU to complete and share with the children. Pick one or two of them and share your own thoughts with the children. Ask the Holy Spirit and share appropriate examples or your testimonies.

- When I think about the throne of God, I feel…
- Thinking of the throne of God helps me when…
- When I stand on the sea of glass I think I will…

Games

Fun Time

- **"Draw it"**

  - As white as a sheet, as white as snow, as wise as an owl.
  - Every fish that gets away appears great.
  - Lips that speak knowledge are a priceless jewel
  - The only reason I like birthdays is because mom gives us loads of ice cream.
  - Don't touch the stinky cheese.
  - The mark of a good leader is loyal followers.

- **Paper Planes**

- **I Found My Dentures!**

- **The Guardian**

Notes

10.1 WALKING IN LOVE
LOVE GOD FIRST

Welcome 5'

Find out about the children. Share your answers first.
- Ask children what they did during the week.
- Find out about children's room.
- Find out if there are windows in their room and what they can see from the windows.

Icebreaker Share your answers first.
- If you could talk to an animal, what animal would you like to talk to and why?
- What would you ask or say to them?

Name The Books 5'

Encourage the children to recite the entire books in the New Testamnent.

Next week we will have Old Testament Extreme Challenge!

EXTREME CHALLENGE!!
Get them all on your own! GET A PRIZE!

MATTHEW, MARK, LUKE, JOHN, ACTS, ROMANS,
1ST & 2ND CORINTHIANS, GLATIANS, EPHESIANS,
PHILIPPIANS, COLOSSIANS, 1ST & 2ND THESSALONIANS,
1ST & 2ND TIMOTHY, TITUS, PHILEMON,
HEBREWS, JAMES, 1ST & 2ND PETER,
1ST, 2ND & 3RD JOHN, JUDE, REVELATION

Process

TEACHER

1) Review the Books
2) Ask for a volunteer to recite alone or with friends.
3) Encourage & reward!

STUDENTS

Say the names of the books in the Bible by yourself and get a sticker!

STICKER PLEASE...

Word: Lesson Objectives

This is the last unit of this book! Commend all of the children for doing a great job! Encourage them to complete three more lessons!

Review

In Unit 2, we talked about how God is omnipotent, omniscient, and omnipresent. Tell me which one goes with these words.
- ○ Let children match the three words.
    - God is powerful. (Omnipotent)
    - God knows everything. (Omniscient)
    - God is everywhere. (Omnipresent)

How does the fact that God is powerful, knows everything, and is everywhere make you feel?
- ○ Share with children how that makes you feel.
- ○ Have the children share how the greatness of God make them feel.

Psalm 139 says God put you together in your mother's body. God knows every bone in your body and He knows how many hairs are on your head.

How does that make you feel?
- ○ Share with children how it makes you feel.
- ○ Have the children share how the verse make them feel.

God knows everything about us, and we can love Him more than anything just by knowing who He is.

Today we are going to talk about loving God first.

One of the Pharisees, who was a teacher of the Law asked Jesus, *"Which is the most important commandment in the Law?" (Matthew 2236)*

Who were the Pharisees?
- ○ Have the children share their answers.

- • The Pharisees were people who tried to be right with God by following those rules.

The Lesson

What is a commandment?

- Have the children share their answers.

- A commandment is an important rule given by God that tells people how to love God and know Him more.

- Some people follow the commandments like rules and regulations.

- Note: The focus of this unit is not on the Ten Commandments, but if children do not know what they are, you can talk about them. (See Exodus 20.)

    1. Do not put any other gods in place of Me.
    2. Do not make statues of gods that look /Jke anything in the sky or on the earth or in the waters. Do not bow down to them or worship them.
    3. Do not misuse the name of the Lord your God The Lord will find gwlty anyone who misuses His name.
    4. Remember to keep the Sabbath day holy
    5. Honor your father and mother. Then you w!II live a long time in the land the Lord your God is giving you.
    6. Do not commit murder.
    7. Do not commit adultery.
    8. Do note steal.
    9. Do not five false witness against your neighbor.
    10. Do not long for anything that belongs to your neighbor.

In your opinion, which one of the commandment is the most important commandment?

- Have the children share their thoughts.

Which commandment do you think Jesus said was the most important?

- Have the children share their thoughts.

- Jesus said that the most important commandment is to love God first. In Matthew 22:37 Jesus answered the Pharisee's question and said:

    "'Love the Lord your God with all your heart and with all your soul.
    Love Him with all your mind' This is the first and most important commandment."

Do you love God?
- Have the children share they feel toward God.

How can we love God?
- Have the children share their ideas.

• Share with the children how you love God.

Let's read Luke 10:38-42:

> Jesus and his disciples went on their way Jesus came to a village where a woman named Martha lived She welcomed him into her home. She had a sister named Mary Mary sat at the Lord's feet listening to what he said But Martha was busy with all the things that had to be done. She came to Jesus and said, "Lord, my sister has left me to do the work by myself Don't you care? Tell her to help me!""Martha, Martha,"the Lord answered. "You are worried and upset about many things. But only one thing is needed. Mary has chosen what is better. And it will not be taken away from her. 11

What are the names of the two sisters in this story?
- Have the children share their answers.

• Martha and Mary are the two sisters.

What was Martha doing?
- Have the children share their answers.

• Martha was busy with all the things that had to be done.

What was Mary doing?
- Have the children share their answers.

• Mary sat at Jesus's feet and listened to Him.

How did Martha feel about Mary sitting by Jesus?
- Have the children share their answers.

• She was upset because Mary was not helping her.

What did Jesus say to Martha?
- Have the children share their answers.

• He told her Mary was not distracted.

• He also said Mary had chosen what is better.

Why do you think Mary chose to be with Jesus?
- Have the children share their thoughts.

• Jesus was just stopping by at their house, and they did not know when He was going to leave.

• Mary chose to spend time with Jesus because she loved Him and wanted to be with Him as much as possible.

When you choose to spend time with someone, it shows that you love that person.
When you choose to spend time with God, it shows that you love Him.

In John 14:15 Jesus said that anyone who loves Him will obey His teaching.
Do you remember we talked about the things God wants us to choose to do? What were they?
God wants us to choose to …

- ○ Have the children fill in the blank.

- • Possible answers: apologize, forgive, obey, serve, give, honor

When you choose to do any of those things, you are showing God that you love Him and that you are putting Him first.

Hebrews 6:10 says:

DRAW A PICTURE

Draw a picture or write a letter to God. Tell God how much you love Him.

Below are sentences for YOU to complete and share with the children. Pick one or two of them and share your own thoughts with the children. Ask the Holy Spirit and share appropriate examples or your testimonies.

- I have difficult time spending time with God when...
- I try to love God first by... (share how you overcome distraction).
- Share how God revealed His love to you when you have spent time with Him. (Where were you? What were you asking God? What did God say to you?)

Games

- **"Scene 1. Take 1"**

 the three little pigs, Moses striking the rock, a gum stuck under a shoe, people playing chess, someone jumping a rope, Israelites marching around the wall of Jericho, a person eating spaghetti and meatball

- **Draw for the Master**

 an elephant waking on a tight rope, a scuba diver encountering a whale, earrings and bracelets on a round table, a parrot eating cucumbers, a man holding an umbrella with holes in it

- **The Secret Object**

- **Masking Tape Activities**

Notes

10.2 WALKING IN LOVE
KEEP CONNECTED TO JESUS

Welcome

Find out about the children. Share your answers first.

- Ask children what they did during the week.
- Find out if children have bought something in a store with their own money.
- Ask how buying something with your money made them feel.

Icebreaker   Share your answers first.

- If you had $500 to spend and give away, what would you do with it?

Name The Books

EXTREME CHALLENGE!!
Get them all on your own! GET A PRIZE!

GENESIS, EXODUS, LEVITICUS NUMBERS,
DEUTRONOMY, JOSHUA, JUDGES, RUTH,
1ST & 2ND SAMUEL, 1ST & 2ND KINGS,
1ST & 2ND CHRONICLES, EZRA, NEHEMIAH,
ESTHER, JOB, PSALMS, PROVERBS, ECCLESIASTES,
SONG OF SOLOMON, ISAIAH, JEREMIAH,
LAMENTATIONS, EZEKIEL, DANIEL, HOSEA,
JOEL, AMOS, OBADIAH, JONAH, MICAH,
NAHUM, HABAKKUK, ZEPHANIAH, HAGGAI,
ZECHARIAH, MALACHI

Encourage the childten to recite the entire books in the Old Testamnent.

Next week we will have Extreme Challenge for the 66 Books in the Bible!!

Process

TEACHER	STUDENTS
1) Review the Books 2) Ask for a volunteer to recite alone or with friends. 3) Encourage & reward!	Say the names of the books in the Bible by yourself and get a sticker!

STICKER PLEASE...

Word: Lesson Objectives

Share with children how you connect with Jesus and share an appropriate testimony of the difference Jesus has made in your life. At the end of the lesson, you will ask children if they would like to make a decision to follow Jesus.

Review

Last week we talked about loving God first.

When we love God, what do we do?

- ○ Have the children share their thoughts.

- • When we love God, we choose to do things God's way.

- • When we love God, we share our thoughts with Him and listen to Him.

In Unit 5 of this book, we learned about talking and listening.

Do you remember learning about sheep recognizing the shepherd's voice?

- ○ Have the children open their activity book to Unit 5, Lesson 1, and see what they have drawn.

Do you remember how Samuel learned to hear God's voice?

- ○ Go to Unit 5, Lesson 2, and look at what you have drawn of Samuel learning to talk with God.

What did Jesus do to be close to God?

- ○ Have the children share their answers.

- • Jesus went to a special quiet place to talk with God.

- • Look at what you drew in Unit 5, Lesson 3.
- ○ Have the children share their pictures.

When have you spent time by yourself with God?

- ○ Share a story of a time when you spent time with God.
- ○ Have the children share their answers.

Let's read John 15:5-8:

> I am the vine. You are the branches. If anyone remains joined to me, and I to him, he will bear a lot of fruit You cannot do anything without me. If anyone does not remain joined to me, he is like a branch that is thrown away and dries up. Branches like those are picked up. They are thrown into the fire and burned

Have you ever seen a branch cut off from a tree?
What happens to a branch that is cut off from a tree or a vine?

- It will die.

Will the branch bear fruit when it is cut off?

- No, it will not bear any fruit.

Have you ever experienced power outages? What happened when the power went out?

- Have the children share their experiences.

Were you able to turn on the TV or use the microwave oven?

- Have the children share their answers.

- When there is a power outage, you cannot turn on the TV or use a microwave oven.

Jesus said that when a branch is cut off from the vine, it cannot bear fruit. Not being connected to Jesus is like having a power outage inside of you. Just the way TVs, microwave ovens, refrigerators, lights, and phones will not work when they are not connected to electricity, so we will not be able to make good choices when we are not connected to Jesus.

When you believe Jesus has put all of your sins on the cross for you, God will forgive your sins, and you will be able to live with Him forever. People who have decided to follow Jesus will talk to Him for the rest of their lives.

- Ask children the following questions to give them an opportunity to make a decision to follow Jesus as their Lord and Savior.
- There is a prayer you can have them repeat on next page.

- Would you like to be connected to Jesus so that you can make good choices?

- Do you feel that Jesus really loves you?

- Do you want your sins to be forgiven?

- Would you like God to forgive you for lying, stealing, getting angry, not lis tening to your parents, not being kind to your siblings or friends, or having a bad attitude?

- Do you believe that Jesus died on the cross so that God could forgive you all of your sins?

- Do you believe Jesus rose from the dead?

If you said "yes" to all of the questions, and would like to follow Jesus, please close your eyes and repeat this prayer after me.

Lord Jesus, I am sorry for all of the bad things I have done. Please forgive me. I believe Je sus died for me so that I could be forgiven and be with You forever. I believe Jesus rose from the dead and that He is alive. Please send Your Holy Spirit into my heart. Holy Spirit, please teach me and guide me so I can make good choices. I love you God. I love you Je sus!

You have made a decision to follow Jesus, and Jesus is so happy that you did!

DRAW A PICTURE

Close your eyes and listen to John Chapter 15 verses 5–8. Draw a picture of these verses.

Share With the Children 5′

Below are sentences for YOU to complete and share with the children. Pick one or two of them and share your own thoughts with the children. Ask the Holy Spirit and share appropriate examples or your testimonies.

- I decided to follow Jesus… (Share when, where, and how.)
- When I am connected to Jesus (spending time with Him) I feel…
- I am so glad I am connected to Jesus because…

Fun Time

Games 10+

- **"Draw it"**

 a diamond, a river, a king, an ornament, a musician, an island, a school, grape juice, star in the east, sandals, Israel, a comb, an afternoon, one hour, a chin, a tongue, a doctor, a cucumber, boots, a car

- **Who/What am I?**

 Fruit: oranges, grapes, raspberry, strawberry, lemon, cherry, peach, banana, melon, watermelon, kiwi, pineapple, apple, mango, pear, blueberries, grapefruit, cantaloupe, limes, apricot

- **Card Games**

- **Super Toes**

10.3 WALKING IN LOVE
FRUITS OF LOVE

Find out about the children. Share your answers first.

- Ask children what they did during the week.
- Find out which store children enjoy going with their parents the most.
- Find out which store children enjoy going with their parents the least.

Icebreaker Share your answers first.

- •If you could own a store what kind of store, what kind of store would you own and why?

Name The Books
5'

Books of the Week

EXTREME CHALLENGE!!
Get them all on your own! GET A PRIZE!

CERTIFICATE OF COMPLETION
This is to certy that _____
has recited the names of
the 66 books in the Bible successfully.
Date _____ Siganture _____

Have the children recite the 66 books in the Bible and sign the certificate.

Process

TEACHER	STUDENTS
1) Ask for a volunteer to recite alone or with friends. 2) Sign the Certificate in children's Activity Book	Say the names of the books in the Bible by yourself and get a certificate!

PLEASE SIGN MY CERTIFICATE

Word: Lesson Objectives

Help children find ways to connect to Jesus to bear good fruit.

The Lesson

<u>Today we are going to talk about fruits we produce.</u>

In Galatians Paul talks about the good fruits and the bad fruits we produce.

What do you think are the fruits of sins?

o   Have the children share their thoughts.

•   Here are the examples: Lies, hate, violence, anger, jealousy, thinking only about yourself, impatience, impure thoughts, teasing, embarrassing others, rudeness, disobedience, dishonoring, causing trouble, not listening, unkind words.

When we are angry, does anything good come out of it?

•   No.

When we dishonor our parents, do we produce kindness?

•   No.

In John 15:1-2, Jesus said:

> *I am the true vine. My Father is the gardener. He cuts off every branch joined to me that does not bear fruit He trims eve!JI branch that doesbear fruit. Then it will bear even more fruit*

What does God the Father do to every branch that does not bear fruit?

o   Have the children share their answers.

•   He cuts off the branches.

What happens to the branches that bear fruit?

o   Have the children share their answers.

•   He trims the branches and they bear more fruit.

John 15:4-Sa says:

> *No branch can bear fruit by itself It must remain joined to the vine. In the same way, you can't bear fruit unless you remain joined to me. I am the vine. You are the branches. If you remain joined to me, and I to you, you will bear a lot of fruit*

Jesus is talking about us connecting to Him and bearing fruit.

What are some ways we connect to Jesus?

o   Have the children share their answers.

•   We connect to Jesus by talking to Him and listening to Him.

Is Jesus talking about the fruits you can eat?
- ○ Have the children share their thoughts.

- • No he is not talking about fruits we eat.

- • He is talking about joy or happiness that people experience as a result of the choices you make.

What do you think the fruits are?
- ○ Have the children share their thoughts.

- • Jesus is saying that when you are connected to Him, you will do things that matters to people around you.

John 15:5b-6, Jesus said:

> You can't do anything without me. If you don't remain joined to me, you are like a branch that is thrown away and dries up. Branches like those are picked up. They are thrown into the fire and burned

Let's read Galatians 5:22-23:

> But the fruit the Holy Spirit produces is love, joy and peace. It is being patient, kind and good It is being faithful and gentle and having control of oneself

What are the fruit of the Holy Spirit?
- ○ Have the children listen to the verses again and accept answers.

What do loving people do?
- ○ Have the children share their thoughts.

What do people full of joy look like?
- ○ Have the children share their thoughts.

What does a person who has peace do?
- ○ Have the children share their thoughts.

Have you ever seen a person who is patient?
- ○ Have the children share their thoughts.

What do you think it means to have self-control?
- ○ Have the children share their thoughts.

Let's play a Game: Answer Yes or No

A person who bears the fruit of love is…
    disobedient. (No.)
    polite to his or her parents. (Yes.)
    a good helper. (Yes.)
    always thinking about him- or herself

A person who bears the fruit of joy is…`
    grumpy. (No.)
    someone who makes people happy. (Yes.)

A person who bears the fruit of peace is…
    not angered easily. (Yes.)
    someone who challenges people. (No.)

A person who bears the fruit of patience…
    argues with people. (No.)
    can wait for a long time. (Yes.) wants things right away. (No.)

A person who bears the fruit of kindness…
    teases friends or siblings. (No.)
    holds doors for people. (Yes.)
    thinks of other people first. (Yes.)

A person who bears the fruit of goodness…
    shares his or her toys. (Yes.)
    does not care about other people. (No.)
    is polite. (Yes.)

A person who bears the fruit of faithfulness…
    tells lies. (No.)
    keeps his or her promises. (Yes.)
    changes his or her mind easily. (No.)

A person who bears the fruit of gentleness…
    can be violent. (No.)
    is careful with things. (Yes.)
    can take care of sick people. (Yes.)

A person who bears the fruit of self-control…
    gets upset easily. (No.)
    can work hard without complaining. (Yes.)
    stop playing video games when they are asked to. (Yes.)

Close your eyes as I speak this over you .

○ Have the children close their eyes as you speak this over them.

- You were created to love God. No one can love God the way you love God.

- You are designed to produce good fruit.

- That means you were created to do great things with God.

- When you keep connecting with Jesus, you will produce good fruit.

- When you choose to do what God wants you to do, you will become who God has created you to be.

Activities

DRAW A PICTURE

Draw a picture of Jesus connected to God and you connected to Jesus.

Draw a picture of yourself producing good fruit.

Share With the Children

5'

Below are sentences for YOU to complete and share with the children. Pick one or two of them and share your own thoughts with the children. Ask the Holy Spirit and share appropriate examples or your testimonies.

- I know I am doing what God wants me to do when…

- Share how the Lord leads you to build other people's life.

- I see the fruit of _____ in…
  (Identify the fruit of each child in your group and encourage them.)

Fun Time

Games

10+

- **Telephone**

  - I'm so sorry. I didn't mean to frighten you. But I was afraid.
  - Be who you really are, do not change for anyone, and always dream big.
  - All you have to do is believe.
  - God has perfect timing. Never early, never late.
  - A cheerful heart brings smile to your face.

- **Paper Planes**

- **I Found My Dentures!**

- **Mission Balance**

- In the last page of each *Splash Zone Children's Activity Book*, you will find the "Certificate of Completion."
- Use this page to acknowledge each child for his/her diligence and congratulate them for completing the *Splash Zone Chtldren's Activity Book*
- Celebrate their accomplishments with the adults in the small group.
- Detach and frame the certificate.

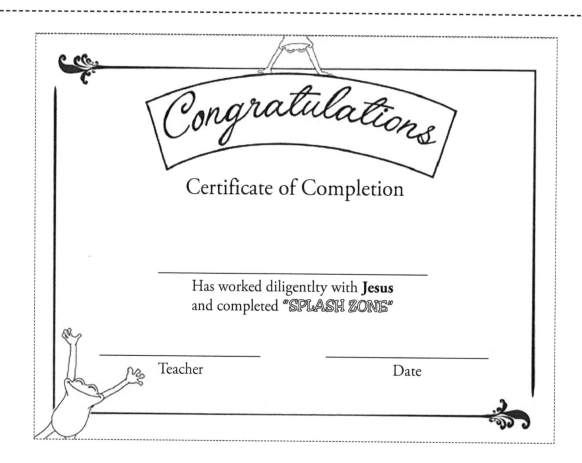

Congratulations

Certificate of Completion

_____

Has worked diligentlty with **Jesus**
and completed "SPLASH ZONE"

_____   _____
Teacher   Date

About the Author

Kazuko developed curriculums and trained instructors for English School at Yamaha Music Co. Ltd., in Tokyo, Japan. She is currently teaching Japanese at Verbling, an online language school.

Kazuko holds Master's Degree in Divinity from Garrett- Evangelical Theological Seminary. She and her husband have led several intergenerational small groups over the years. Splash Zone was developed through this experience and passion to share God's heart for the generations.

CPSIA information can be obtained
at www.ICGtesting.com
Printed in the USA
LVHW011651140423
744405LV00030B/324